The Harmony of Science and the Scriptures

The Harmony of Science and Scripture

By

Harry Rimmer, D.D., Sc.D.

WM. B. EERDMANS PUBLISHING COMPANY
Grand Rapids Michigan

John Laurence Frost
Memorial Library

Volume One

THE HARMONY OF SCIENCE AND SCRIPTURE

By Harry Rimmer, D.D., Sc.D.

ISBN 0-8028-1554-5

Twenty-second printing, September 1973

PRINTED IN THE UNITED STATES OF AMERICA

Foreword

THE matter contained in this volume of apologetics has been delivered in lecture form before hundreds of audiences and student groups, totalling many thousands of auditors. Some of this matter has been circulated in the form of pamphlets, many hundreds of thousands of copies having been distributed in a simplified form. The author has revised this material and has put it in this permanent form, that it might be available to libraries and schools that require this type of apologetics.

This is the first of six volumes, to appear at intervals. These volumes will constitute a library of apologetics and Christian evidences which is dedicated to the memory of John Laurence Frost. This young man, who faced triumphantly and victoriously all the problems that meet a Christian student on the modern campus, was called home to be with Christ just before his prospective graduation from Stanford University. His parents, in appreciation of the aid to his Christian life that this type of material had been, are pleased to erect this memorial to him. They do this not only in remembrance of their son, but they thus aspire also to extend his influence in the lives of countless others.

The book is not dedicated, and these words are only in appreciation of a life that the author knew to be transformed by the grace of God as it is manifested through Jesus Christ.

HARRY RIMMER.

Contents

Chapter *Page*

Modern Science and the First Fundamental

CHAPTER I

Modern Science and the First Fundamental

EVERY generation not only faces its own problems and difficulties, but also erects its own standards of values and judgment. So the average man of the twentieth century has a new measure by which he computes the value of all things, material, philosophical, or spiritual. Being taught from early childhood to think largely in the terms of science, it is inevitable that modern man should reply to every problem which challenges his interest, "What does science say on this subject?"

In these most stirring and fascinating days of renewed inquiry, when all the old things are being weighed once again in new scales, it is only natural that the judgment of science will be sought even upon the basic premises of our religious philosophy. In the minds of past generations it would have been utterly impossible to raise this question of the scientific evaluation of spiritual things, as it was the general opinion in the age that has closed that the Bible was the final voice in all matters and subjects of discussion. Our generation, in turn, has raised the fetish of science, to which we bow down and worship with a blind faith unknown to the credulous age that is commonly called "the age of Bible believers". Reverence has not been displaced in the hearts of men. It has rather sought a new object for its veneration. So in that sturdier generation when a more robust faith ruled the minds of men who had not yet bent the knee to the Baal of supposed scholarship and prejudiced research, this question would never have been considered and this chapter would never have been written.

We must hasten to remark that we in no wise regret the new order or the present age. The contrary is rather the fact. If the Bible is true and if its revelations are indeed from Almighty God, we need not fear to have it tested by any standard of truth that is honest, and that is established. If the words of the Great Book are not in full accord with all known *fact,* then we have been mistaken in calling it the Word of God. We use the word "fact" in its accepted meaning, as distinct from theory and unproved hypotheses.

Our main objection to the pseudo-scientific philosophy of this present generation is that it manifests an amazing willingness to surrender the eternal verity of God's revelation for the unfounded theories propounded by men who are utterly without ability to prove their wild imaginings. And science, we must repeat, is a correlated body of absolute knowledge. The accumulation of reliable scientific knowledge is a gradual and slow process. The trial and error method is perhaps the most prominent in all scientific techniques! Generation after generation discards the conclusions of their predecessors, until finally a new stratum is laid upon the slowly accumulating pyramid of unquestioned and unquestionable fact.

The Book which men call the Bible has remained unchanged and undeviating for thousands of years. Its writers never contradict one another, and all of its contents has an unwavering unanimity upon every subject introduced into its marvelous pages. We are perfectly willing to have the contents of this Book tested by science, as by any other established standard. We would unhesitatingly state that when men of science agree unanimously upon any correlated body of facts and do not change their conclusions or agreements concerning these facts for several thousand years, we will then be willing, if necessary, to discard the Bible and accept their conclusions instead! We think that this is but an honest test, since the Bible rests upon that pedestal of millenniums of unchanging and unvarying agreement. Sometimes we are forced to realize that we live in an age which, priding itself upon the term "scientific", is extremely superficial in many of its philosophical conclusions.

As an illustration, the author would recount an experience that occurred when he was delivering a course of addresses at one of our colleges. After one particular lecture, we were approached by a young student who desired to enter into a discussion concerning origins. This young inquirer began by saying, "I would like to talk to you in the language of science. In this interview I hope we can confine ourselves to scientific facts and language and get to the bottom of this question I desire to ask of you."

Of course we were more than willing to meet the youth upon his chosen grounds. Our early days in the study of medicine were spent learning double-jointed, twelve cylinder, knee-action words, and we felt that if he wanted to speak exclusively in the weird and compound verbiage of science, we should be happy to accommodate him. We felt that the discussion promised much.

The lad opened the conversation by saying, "Where did the world come from?" To this the writer replied, "Now, let us be scientific. What do you mean by 'world'? Do you mean this planet, this solar system, the sidereal system, the universe, the cosmos, or what?"

In some surprise the boy hesitated, then with an embarrassed smile replied with an expressive wave of his hands, "I mean the whole blame shooting match."

We laughed and said, "That's not scientific, but it is very clear. You wish to know where the cosmos came from."

He said, "All right, if that's the word I want; where *did* the cosmos come from?"

"It was created."

"By whom, or by what?"

"By God," was our simple and sincere reply.

"Who or what is God?" he asked.

We looked at him closely, to be sure he was really in earnest with this question. We saw, at least, that he thought he was thinking, and even that attitude on the part of a student is one to be encouraged! So we answered, "God is the Deity Who made all things. You may call Him 'First Cause', 'Logos', 'Personified Power', or whatever else you wish. The point is, behind the appearance of the cosmos there remains a Person Who is the Author of all created things. He is Life Inherent."

"All right," he said, "we will pass that for a moment and ask this: "Who made God?"

"Nobody made God," was our rejoinder. "You are not being scientific in your language. We said that God was Life Inherent. In the universe there are but two types of life. *Creature* life is life that is transmitted. The life of Deity is life that is inherent, thus establishing by existence per se, a Creator. We said that He was self-existent, and there is no other term for an Infinity that is personified that is more expressive than Inherent Being. God always was, for there could be no beginning to Deity."

"Oh, come," he said, "I can't accept that, you know. It's not scientific."

We said, "I am sorry you can't see that, but that's the best we can do. Now let me ask you some questions, to which we also wish a scientific answer. Where do *you* think the cosmos came from?"

"It was evolved."

"Out of what?"

"Out of a nebulous mass of gaseous matter."

Fortunately, we had read this same textbook, and so we were prepared to ask, "Where did this nebulous mass of gaseous matter come from?"

The young man frowned in puzzlement for a moment and said, "Oh, I guess you would say that was created."

"But I am through talking now. Where do *you* say that it came from?"

"Well, I will concede that the original mass of vapor was created."

"By Whom, or by what, was it created?"

"By Nature."

"Very well, then, what or who is Nature?"

He hesitated a moment and said, "Er, you know, Nature is the — er, by Nature we mean what we mean when we say *Nature!*"

We said, "I am afraid that is not very scientific nor clear. We do not know Nature. Just who is it?"

"Well, Nature is the first cause of everything, the primary beginning."

"Then who made Nature and when did Nature begin?"

The lad flung open his hands in despair at our stupidity and said, "Nobody made Nature at any time; Nature always was!"

We laughed and said, "I am sorry. I cannot accept that; it is not scientific!" There we parted company, both of us having been talking about the same identical Person or Force under two different names.

The man who thinks his way through the mechanics of creation will find, behind all created matter, a Personified Being of intelligence and power. This Being he calls God.

The man who is content to be superficial and only dimly grasp at the appearance of reason behind matter, is content to say, "Nature," and pass on.

Unfortunately, in such discussions as the foregoing a vital law of logic is disregarded or violated. As Dr. Harris Gregg has so thoughtfully reasoned, it is a simple and profitable matter to discuss problems of origin with any person who has in his philosophy and logic an A and a Z. By A, we mean that point beyond which a man's mind cannot reason in the direction of beginnings. We have to start with something. Whatever it is that we start with is our A. The Z in the alphabet of logic is that point in the future, beyond which the mind cannot travel with clarity. We have to stop somewhere, and the stopping point is our Z.

It is utterly impossible to have a logical discussion without first announcing the A and the

Z. It is only possible to think in a straight line if we think between two objectives. The man who seeks to reason without an A and a Z in the alphabet of his logic reminds us of a playful Airedale dog who for many years was our companion and friend. This dog was very fond of exercise and fun, and if there was nobody around to play with, he had a game that he played in solitude. He would start after his tail, and go round in a circle: like a man reasoning with no A and no Z! The dog, however, had one advantage. As he went around in these endless circles, *he was careful to keep his end in view!* The man, however, who reasons this way has no end to keep in view, and his mental exercise is more fruitless than the physical exercise of the dog.

So this writer would be careful to announce that as he starts on his pilgrimage of philosophical reasoning, he begins with God. When he has thought his way as far back in the nebulous dimness of the beginning of all things as a mind can feel its way, he *starts* with a God already existent, unlimited in power. Back of God we cannot go. Of course we cannot think before Him Who is infinite and eternal. In our philosophy He is the very start of timeless age and eternal beginnings.

When we have journeyed as far down the vista of the future as the human mind can go, we *end* with God. The human mind can only stagger on its questing way as far into the coming eternities as it can envision God. So in our philosophy, Deity is the beginning and the end for us, our Alpha and Omega, the starting point and termination as well.

Having then settled, for the sake of clarity, the fact that we must in logic begin with God, we will turn to the realm of logic and science, to see if His Person can be demonstrated by independent, external evidence.

The first fundamental of the Christian faith is this: that God is a Person. The fact of deity is universally conceded by all save the fool, who "hath said in his heart, there is no God." This traditional and foundational tenet of all faiths is found in false and true philosophy alike. Even those who would becloud the issue with nebulous evasions of fact, speak of the existence of a deity, even though they postulate it as some ethereal and unknowable force or principle. The Christian revelation, however, goes right to the heart of the matter with a plain annunciation of the most vital fact in the thought of the human race, namely: *There is a God Who is a Person!*

This was the reason for the coming of Christ. Jesus clothed Himself in human flesh that He might manifest God. He stated that the purpose of His coming was that He, Jesus, might show forth God. The Only Begotten Son, Who was in the bosom of the Father from eternity, clothed Himself with the habiliments of temporal existence, that He might teach the reality, the Personality, and the certainty of God's being. Upon this foundation of the Personality of God, the entire Christian structure rests.

Turning then to the realm of science and reason to see what the basic foundational facts of science might say as to the existence of God, we will appeal to an unvarying law of logic. This law is, "Begin with a fact that is universally conceded and reason from that fact to your conclusion." So at the start of this investigation we must ask the reader to grant a concession. That concession being granted, we will demonstrate each successive step as we press on to the scientific evaluation of the credibility and reality of the existence of God.

The concession that we desire is simply this: That there is a cosmos!

This fact no reasoning mind can deny.

The universe is real.

The solar system is concrete.

The planet on which we live, and which is the source and scene of most of our scientific investigation, is a stubborn, indisputable, unchanging, irrefutable fact.

Now then, beginning with the certainty of the fact of the cosmos, we raise the eternal question, "Whence?" We do not live in a world made up of a single ball of solid matter. We are part of a marvelous and complex system. Not only does the sun, which is the source of our earthly light, revolve as the nucleus of a solar system, but this system is itself part of a universe. This universe in turn is one of many such that make up the physical cosmos. We are a tiny but integral part of a complex physical creation. Three hundred and fifty million solar systems are reported with their suns, planets, and satellites in our galaxy. Then beyond all this, the spiral nebulae are seen as silver snails in the garden of God, each of them being so vast in diameter that they are at present beyond the reach of our counting devices!

Reason doth rear her head and cry, "Here it is, this marvelous and amazing cosmos. Whence did it all come?"

It is kindergarten logic to reply that you cannot get more out of anything than you have previously put in. We think it will be conceded as a principle that out of nothing you get naught. Also, out of something you get no more than that thing is able to contain. You cannot take a gallon of milk out of a pint bottle unless you refill the bottle again and again. You cannot put a hundred dollars in the bank and take out a thousand. (Indeed, in these tragic years of the depression you are something of a wizard if you can get out what you put in!). The man who seeks to take out of the bank far more than he put in will find himself a more or less grateful recipient of free board and room for many months to come. This, then, is a fundamental point of logical reasoning. We recognize that out of nothing, nothing comes.

Now, add to that what Hull, of Dartmouth,

calls "the fundamental law of physics". This expresses the case perfectly in scientific terms. This law may be stated in these words: "All transformations of matter that result in the production of energy are a result of degeneration: a breaking down from the complex to the simple."

As an illustration of this unquestionable scientific fact, we would introduce the complex, highly organized material that is called petroleum. This petroleum is put through what is called a "cracking process". This process results in the degeneration or breaking down of the original mass into its simpler component ingredients. Out of the complex mass called petroleum, an almost innumerable list of substances will be derived — kerosene, benzine, gasoline, various grades of lubricating oils, vaseline, and greases — all produced in the breaking down and shattering of the amazingly complex structure of petroleum.

One of these simpler ingredients we call gasoline. This gasoline is introduced into a manifold which gasifies this substance, in which form it is put into the cylinder of an internal combustion engine. This compressed matter is energized by an electrical spark and is further degenerated by an explosion. In the course of its final destruction by flame, power is imparted to the piston of the engine, and the exhaust gases are wasted on the atmosphere. *Through this process of degeneration, however, power and motion are created!*

Now then, in all of the physical universe all motion, power, and energy are the result of degeneration. In the entire universe the opposite process is never seen. Nowhere in physics do we see a natural tendency to build up from the simple to the complex. Therefore Hull's conclusion is "that no matter what your theory of creation may be, you have to start with a universe already charged with a tremendous amount of high-grade energy, like a clock that has been wound up and started and has been running down ever since."

In the light of this view of the universe, the logical question to ask is, "Who wound it up?"

The clearest discussion of this problem of the whence of physical matter was presented to us one evening by a little lad who perhaps did not realize that fools may ask questions that the wise cannot answer. In this case, however, he challenged our interest by the rather abrupt query, "In all the whole world, how many different kinds of things are there?"

His mother interrupted to say, "You don't need to answer that question, doctor; I didn't know what he was going to ask you;" but we said that we would like to try to answer that question.

Turning to the lad, we said, "Freddie, I don't know much, but I happen to know that. In all the whole world, the heaven, the earth, all the stars and suns and moons and planets, there are less than one hundred different things."

The lad looked at us in amazement and said, "Aw, you must be spoofing me. I know there are more than a million, because I know a million different things myself."

Matching his seriousness with a like mien, we replied, "Now let's examine this and see. You can't know a million different things, for in all the universe there are only ninety-six different things, which are called 'elements'."

The lad shook his head with stubbornness and said, "I know there are more than that!"

Entering into the spirit of the argument, we said, "All right, what is one of those things that you know?"

Being in sight of the supper table, he said, "Well, salt is one thing."

That one was easy. We said, "No, Freddie, salt is not one thing; salt is two things. Somebody has taken a piece of metal called sodium and a piece of a gas called chlorine, and mixed the two things together. The result is what chemists call 'sodium chloride' and we common folks call 'salt'. But salt is not one thing; it is two things in combination."

"How about water? That's one thing!"

"No, water is two things. Two pieces of a gas called hydrogen and one piece of a gas called oxygen are mixed together, and they make water."

"How about air? Isn't *that* one thing?"

"Wrong again. Air is always three things. Seventy-nine pieces of a gas called nitrogen mixed with twenty-one pieces of a gas called oxygen, with a tiny, tiny portion of carbonic acid gas, make up the simplest kind of air. Air is not one thing. It might be as many as twelve or fourteen things, depending on how close you live to a glue factory or a garbage dump!"

The boy laughed with keen appreciation and said, "Oh, I see! It is kind of like arithmetic, or like the alphabet."

That is the perfect figure of creation. The whole world of mathematics resolves itself into two divisions. First, we have the factors that men call the numerals. These factors are figures from one to nine, with the cipher added for convenience in multiplication. With these ten factors, combined with intelligence, we can solve the problems of mathematics, and arrive at the solution of the most intricate of these problems. Mathematics, then, are predicated first upon factors, and secondly upon intelligence to manipulate those factors! The science of figures would be utterly impossible without intelligence of a high order, capable of making absolutely innumerable combinations of the few factors. The universe, then, is a combination of factors on purely mathematical formulae. These factors number ninety-six. But factors alone cannot be resolved into mathematics. Intelligence is the more important element in the juggling and arranging of these factors. The entire physical creation is a solved problem in mathematics, for these various elements are combined in different proportions to make up all the intricacy of the physical creation.

The same is true in the world of literature. In the English language we have twenty-six factors, called the alphabet. When these twenty-six letters are manipulated by intelligence of a sufficiently high order, literature is the result. The twenty-six factors by themselves remain dead. When they are combined by intelligence into orderly sequences, they then become a "Gettysburg Address" or a "Twenty-third Psalm." These same factors may be framed by intelligence into "A Message to Garcia"; or they may declare war upon some foreign power. Again, they may be recast into treaties of peace and documents of eternal fidelity. But no matter what the purpose and intent of the expressions of literature may be, there can be no literature until there is intelligence directed to the manipulation of the factors.

The Creator has as the basis of His mathematics, ninety-six figures instead of ten. These figures may be arranged and rearranged again and again into all of the marvelous and ponderable structures that we call the physical universe.

Or shall we say that the Creator has as His alphabet of creation, ninety-six letters at His disposal? As an illustration of this, we take one small series of alphabetical symbols and put them together in this form: STAR. The connotations of that assembling of factors are very definite and concrete and real. Those four symbols, thus arranged, open to us all of the unfathomable vistas of the realm called astronomy.

Now, without changing the value of those factors, we rearrange them into new positions and put them in this order: RATS. At once the mind is struck with the ludicrous nature of this contrast. There is as wide a difference between the orbs of sidereal space and the rodents of a dark and gloomy basement as there is between any two extremes that the human mind can frame. But we have expressed those two extremes by our intelligence, through a simple rearrangement of the factors.

Once more we rearrange this figure, and now it is ARTS. In this new order these tiny creatures spring into our intelligence with all the world of beauty and wonder that is open to the finer side of the human nature. Herein we have music and sculpture, painting and drama, poetry and prose, and all the finer things that make life worth while.

Again we recast these symbols and they become TARS. Can there be a wider gulf in the meaning of words than that which exists between the black, foul-smelling, viscous masses that form the tars, and the ethereal, kinesthetic values of the realm of the arts?

So with this one simple demonstration, which might be multiplied into a thousand, we would show that intelligence by the use of the same identical factors may express widely divergent conceptions.

To apply our illustration, one of the factors in creation is a little letter or symbol called carbon. When the atom of carbon is arranged in a sentence of creation so that each atom is touched at every point by four other atoms, that word spells "diamond".

As we did in the case of the little word "star", we now rearrange the relationship of the atoms of carbon one to another, and changing the pattern, the little word becomes "graphite". The first substance we wear on our person with pride and enjoyment, as the highest and richest adornment that a person can afford. The second we use in our lead pencil to record our casual and passing fancies.

Once again we rearrange the order of this element, and it becomes coal to burn in the furnace. We change it again and it becomes clay. It becomes the substance out of which dishes and pottery may be made.

We may, then, resolve our conclusion into this very simple phrase, "The physical creation is a mathematical organization of certain factors combined upon known and tested formulae."

This raises the next question in the realm of logic: Who is this Combiner? There are surprisingly few answers to this question that reason can even ponder. There is only one answer that reason can accept.

Only the thoughtless, and those who are utterly lacking in logic, can reply, "*Chance* is the combiner of the factors of creation." The statement that life began with a "fortuitous combination of accidental circumstances" and started a process of development and gradual change, is not acceptable to a thinking and reasoning creature. Since the factors of the physical structure are known, and since we recognize the fact that they cannot be manipulated without intelligence into the mathematical formulae and combinations of geometric intricacy, *chance is utterly ruled out.*

We might as well say that success in solving mathematical problems depends upon luck. How many times would it be necessary, let us say, to cast the ten factors of mathematics from a dice box on to a table, before accident arranged these little symbols into the proper answer to a problem in higher mathematics? The solution of a problem in calculus would not be arrived at in a hundred million years of incessant casting forth of the factors of that problem, if the entire matter were left to chance.

Can chance solve an equation?

Can chance add a simple column of figures, or multiply seven figures by six others and find the right solution? If mathematics depended upon luck or accident, we are quite sure that many of us would have had better marks in this fascinating subject in the days of our student experience. Whatever else our conclusion may be concerning the origin of matter, we may well rule out the theory of chance.

We may as well say that literature is the product of chance, as to ascribe creation to that source! How many times do you suppose we would have to put the twenty-six elements of the English language into a hat and shake them out on to a table, before they would shape themselves into an "Evangeline", or fall accidentally into the arrangement of "A Midsummer Night's Dream"? The suggestion is utterly preposterous. Chance is ruled out.

Who, then, is the combiner?

Seeking to evade the only logical conclusion, another man may say, "Recognizing that the universe is a combination of known factors, we believe that law is the combiner."

This author would be the last to deny the presence of law in the natural universe. We would point the reader's attention, however, to the fact that law is predicated upon two postulates. There is no law without a legislator or a legislature. The first requisite for law is the presence of a body, or being, of sufficient authority to *enact* the law.

Law, however, remains inactive until there is, secondly, a police power of sufficient authority to enforce the law that has been enacted. Occasionally we have been in desert places where there was no law. The only guide for conduct was the desire of the individual. Because there was no person or body of authority over that sphere, or none within sufficient reach to enforce the nominal authority, the only law was the ability of the individual to enforce his own paramount desires. It might be said that in those regions the law consists of six statutes, bound in one volume by the Colt Manufacturing Company! The only court of appeal was Judge Winchester, carried in the arm of the appellant. This condition is possible only where there is no organized body with authority to enact and enforce the law of that land. When a wilderness is too far removed from the governing authority, laws may not be enforced therein.

So again we say that it may not be questioned that there is law in the physical universe, and that such law is implacably enforced. There is a law of gravity. Break it, and injury will follow without mercy. The judgments of the cosmos when its laws are broken are instant and inescapable, and these laws speak with clarion tongue of the great Power Who enacted them and keeps them in force.

What is this Power?

Whence is its authority?

Is it derived from the consent of the governed universe?

Not at all!

Natural law is extraneous to the universe that it governs.

There is no greater or more logical argument for the existence of dominating intelligence behind creation, than the very fact of law in nature.

Law, however, is a *creature,* and never a *creator.* Therefore when we seek for the personality of the combining agency that has wrought this stupendous creation out of ninety-six elements mathematically aligned, the term "law" will not satisfy the truly logical inquirer.

Some seek to find an easy way out by the use of the nebulous term, "nature", as did the student whose conversation we recorded at the beginning of this chapter. We recognize the existence of the world of nature, and believe that we can later offer a definition of the word "nature" that will meet with the acquiescence of the thoughtful reader. It cannot, however, be advanced that nature is a creator.

Nature is itself a postulate. The only truly great scientist who ever sought seriously to define nature begins his definition with the very familiar statement, "Nature is that blind, unreasoning force that creates without intelligence . . . " and thus disqualifies nature as a creator!

Can we have creation without intelligence?

Yes, when the parts of an automobile will produce themselves and assemble themselves into a finished and perfect car without aid or direction. We can have creation without intelligence when an airplane will put itself together and fly across the Atlantic with no human help or guidance, or when a giant bridge builds itself across some vast chasm without the aid of engineers and mathematicians!

Why will the human mind always seek to evade an issue that does not coincide with its individual prejudices? The clear-cut issue that we face here is the fact of a mathematical problem, solved by intelligence, in the vast realm of the cosmos. If the universe is a combination of these ninety-six elements, and we have the courage to face the issue squarely, we see that intelligence is as much demanded as are the physical factors themselves.

It is impossible to postulate intelligence apart from personality. We cannot logically conceive of intelligence as a sort of gas permeating the ether of space. Intelligence not only must be personified; it also must be localized.

To meet this issue squarely and to set the matter clearly before the reader, we would suggest this resulting equation: Matter equals creation. Creation equals intelligence. Intelligence equals personality. Personality equals God, which is q. e. d!

That is all that we started out to show!

Logic demands the existence of an intelligent, personified Being, Whom men call God. Simply and clearly, men of courage face the issue squarely and confess this fact: Behind the mathematical perfection of combinations that constitute the universe, there is a Person, Whom we call Deity.

Thus logic demands the very Personality that the Scripture describes and that the evidences of science attest: The visible things of creation have ever argued, to the logic of thinking creatures, the existence of an invisible Creator. This conclusion we cannot escape. So the next query must be, "Does science sustain what logic establishes?" Indeed it does! And we believe that this is a statement that is very easy to establish.

We deal here with Siamese triplets rather than twins. The three aspects of this matter cannot be divorced. Logic demands, Scripture states, and science attests, the living personality of an omnipotent Creator.

When the Apostle Paul addressed the vast concourse of thinkers on Mars Hill in the very center and stronghold of philosophy in his day, he took for his theme this question: "Can a man find God?" This question the great Apostle answered in the affirmative. He then produced a seven-fold argument from the physical creation to sustain his affirmative answer.

Yet in the day of Paul the Apostle, men possessed none of the vast scientific knowledge that is ours today. The world in which we live teems with myriads of evidences of the existence and manifestations of a God Who is a Person. If Paul in his day could produce seven known and tested physical facts which demonstrated the existence of God, it is not too much for us to say that we can produce seven hundred!

This union of science and Scripture is really inevitable. If we grant the existence of an intelligent Creator Who is responsible for the creation of intelligent creatures, it is to be expected that He would seek to make some revelation of Himself *to* His creatures.

This the Creator indeed has done. There is a two-fold revelation of God spread out in majestic array before every inquirer of our generation. The first and the simplest of those revelations is in the realm that men call nature. Nature is really the compilation of the facts of the physical universe that science has made. The visible works of God are seen, studied, analyzed, correlated, and the resultant body of knowledge is called nature.

It is in this arrangement of established facts that the presence of God is most clearly seen. Every realm of pure science ultimately leads men back to the fact of God and His existence, and ushers the careful inquirer into His presence.

We remember an experience that occurred a good many years ago in the classroom in college, when we were listening more or less attentively to the day's study in a class in biology. It had been our fortunate experience to spend the days of our youth in the mountains, where we lived close to what men call nature. Of books we had few, but the creatures of botany, and all the vast world of zoology, were our rather intimate and daily companions. Therefore we had some difficulty, on occasion, in accepting the things that were written in textbooks!

In this class in biology, we remember, the

professor was lecturing that day on his favorite subject. Whenever this good gentleman lacked an explanation of some mystery in the realm of biology, he fell back upon the good old word, "instinct". On this occasion, as he was describing some fascinating fact of biological importance, one of the students asked him for the basic explanation, and automatically the good professor said, "Instinct".

Upon which another student asked, "Doctor, what is instinct?"

The professor said, "Instinct is inherited memory."

Unfortunately, we were present in the class only in a physical sense. Most of our mind was out where the fishing was better! But with half an ear we heard the answer, and without conscious thought, audibly said, "Uh-huh".

This good doctor truly loved an argument in the class and always encouraged such, so with vast glee he pounced upon this unwise rejoinder. Leveling a finger in our direction, he said, "What do you mean, uh-huh?"

Not wishing to become the cynosure of attention, we said, "Excuse me, doctor, I wasn't thinking."

With great delight the doctor nodded and said, "Not an uncommon phenomenon in this class! Nevertheless, when I said that instinct is inherited memory, you spoke up in the negative. Now, sir, can you defend your position?"

We replied, "Yes, I think the position is defensible. I can give, at least, an illustration of a case of instinct that is not attributed to inherited memory.'' So as an instance we recalled to the doctor's mind the strange conduct of a tiny spider very common on the North Pacific coast. This small creature is not much bigger than an ordinary shoe-button, but she makes her nest in the empty shell of any bivalve, from that of a large clam to one of a gigantic abalone.

This tiny spider has a remarkable technique of construction and rearrangement in the establishment of her home. She swings this shell, lying discarded in the vicinity, by two strong silken cables to the overhanging bough of some low shrub. This shell must be lifted from twelve to twenty inches above the ground, that she may rear her brood in safety. The raising of this comparatively enormous mass of material is an engineering problem that can be comprehended only when we graduate it to the ratio of humanity. The spider weighs a fraction of an ounce; the shell may weigh a half a pound. To show you her problem, we would give you this suggestion. If you had to raise thirty-six hundred tons of concrete and steel eighteen hundred feet in the air, how would you do it? You say, "I couldn't do it." Yes, you could, if you had sufficient scientific knowledge and engineering technique. The problem is solved by the spider by true engineering ingenuity, and by an application of a scientific principle.

Somewhere this spider has learned the law of physics that a drying object will shrink and contract. So she locates her shell in relation to her bough and swings down, leaving behind her a thread as wet as she can make it. This thread she ties to one edge of the shell and waits for it to dry. The contraction of this drying thread raises this shell a tiny bit from the ground. The spider then swings down and puts another thread to the opposite edge of the shell and allows that to dry. Laboring thus incessantly without rest day or night, day after day, she spins innumerable threads. Thus raising one edge after the other, perhaps a few microns at a time, she gradually swings that shell into the position that she has selected. With superhuman patience, this busy artificer then spins her threads into a strong, united cable, until two slender ropes support her future home. She then lines the shell with silk, spins a waterproof covering over the whole, and cuts a tiny door in the outside. Entering into this home that ingenuity and patience have contrived, she settles down to rear her brood in peace and safety.

When we had reminded the good doctor of this interesting but well known phenomenon, we asked the question, "How did this spider know that a drying thread would shrink and contract, and raise that shell?"

The professor replied, "That's instinct."

We said, "And instinct is inherited memory?"

The professor said, "That's right."

We then asked. "That means. then. that the

spider inherited this knowledge from the mother, and the mother from the grandmother, and so on back to the first spider that did this?" The professor nodded agreement to this inevitable conclusion.

"Then, sir", we said, "if all this is inherited memory, one spider learning it from the preceding generation, *the first spider that ever did this sat down and figured it out!*" There can be no other conclusion. If instinct is inherited memory, then the first of every species and order that possesses this innate wisdom so remarkable in the world of biology, had the intelligence to study these laws and master them by reason.

With a humorous gesture of resignation, the professor said, "It seems in this case that my definition will not hold up. Now, having upset *my* definition, perhaps you can tell us what instinct really is."

Fortunately, we did not have to search for an answer, as we had thought this thing out in the quietness of the fields, as we correlated the facts of nature to the pages of God's Word.

"Instinct," we maintained, "is imparted wisdom. In the very dawn of creation, the Creator imparted to every creature the knowledge essential to survival in its own environment."

With that conclusion logic can find no fault, nor can science marshal one fact in refutation!

Dogs, for instance, may learn many tricks and perform them to perfection, but the memory of them is never inherited by the puppies that are born from these accomplished parents. Each puppy must in turn be painstakingly trained to learn the same trick over again, and "inherited memory" falls down here.

This case of the spider is just one case among the multiplied thousands of evidences of imparted wisdom that might be mentioned to demonstrate the amazing intelligence planted in the creatures that constitute the realm that men call nature. But this case demonstrates that there is a mind which controls even the minutiae of life. In nature we veritably see the workings and the presence of an omniscient, omnipotent, and omnipresent God.

At least, this has been the testimony of the ages as far back as written records go.

When Abraham dwelt in Ur of the Chaldees, he saw the wonders of God in nature. When David, the Psalmist, smote his harp in the quiet hush of the Judean hills, he sang, "The heavens declare the glory of God, and the firmament showeth the work of his fingers."

So much of God in nature did David see, that without any of our modern astronomical learning the psalmist could say of the sun, "His reins are gone out through all the earth." This is absolutely cold fact!

The earth would go hurtling off into the uttermost bounds of unlimited space, there to crash with some other vast body and thus perish, if the sun did not guide it on its orbit and hold it in place with invisible reins.

The Bible, which owes none of its power or value to purely natural sources, teems with such references to the presence of God in the organized universe, the knowledge of which we call nature.

The language of the stars is understood by every nation of men on all the face of the earth, as they testify of the presence of God in the cosmos. Indeed, it is contended by those children of Abraham who have descended through Ishmael, that it was through this natural revelation that Abraham was called to follow God. The Bible simply says that God called Abraham out of Ur of the Chaldees, while the verbal history of the East purports to tell us how.

According to this old tradition, the father of Abraham was an astrologer in the courts of the Chaldees, and foretold coming events by the stars. He had trained the boy Abraham in such knowledge of the constellations as was possessed by his school. When the older man retired at night and took his ease, he left the young Abraham to lie upon the couch on the flat roof all night, watching the stars for unusual signs and auguries. When such appeared, it was the duty of the boy to call his father, the astrologer, who would seek to read the meaning of the message in the heavenly bodies.

As the young man studied the movements of these bright witnesses night after night through the advancing years, we are told, he noticed that these constellations and bodies seemed to move in obedience to inevitable law. He observed that they apparently wheeled and changed formation on some plan, in response to some intelligent will. Reasoning from this, Abraham thought his way through to the God Who called him to be the father of a new nation. We cannot vouch for the historicity of this record, of course, as it is among the traditions of the East, but tradition often serves as the wings that Truth takes to herself to rise from the ground when crushed by forgetfulness.

It is probably more nearly true to say that Abraham learned to worship God and to believe through the ministry of Melchisedec, who was the priest of monotheism and the prophet of God. The two were friends, and we know that Melchisedec received the tithes from Abraham, as the representative of God and as His minister. We quote this interesting legend only to emphasize the fact that these races and tribes of the desert are sensible to the influence of the stars as a contributing factor to human faith in deity, and even in these marvelous days of scientific erudition, we can still hear the cry of that great astronomer, who saw so much that he exclaimed in wonder, *"Truly, the undevout astronomer is mad!"*

Natural science is the interpretation of the physical universe by the observations of trained men. A "naturalist" is simply an ordinary human being whose eyes are open, and who sees what he looks at! Most of us rarely see what we look at, — or perhaps it would be better to say that we do not observe what we see! The scientist, however, has been trained actually to see facts, to recognize them as such, and to correlate them in their relation with one another. Between scientists and various schools of science, there is not any disagreement concerning the *facts* of nature; the only disagreements are concerning *the interpretations of those facts.*

The plain and unvarnished facts of nature all testify to the reality and presence of God in His creation. The distortion of these facts is the saddest evidence of the illogical method of atheism. Only the blind, or wilfully dishonest, can enter into the study of science, accept things as they are, and doubt the existence of God. Even the eminent agnostic, Huxley, confesses himself "utterly unable to conceive matter if there were no Mind to feature that existence."

That science demonstrates the existence of God is the clear testimony of many eminent men of science. In a recent book, "The Strength of Religion as Shown by Science", Dr. Charles E. deM. Sajous takes as his main thesis, "SCIENCE DEMONSTRATES THE EXISTENCE OF GOD." It does indeed. Sajous states:

> "The creation of matter, of the universe, of the solar system, of the earth and all living things, including ourselves, imposes the need of God in the whole physical domain, the cosmos, to account for *any* of the phenomena known to us."

Call the roll of the American Association for the Advancement of Science, and among the fifteen thousand members you can scarce find a man who will confess himself an atheist. A company of the most eminent of them, headed by Dr. Millikan, who attained fame long before he isolated the atom, recently sent forth a signed statement to the press, declaring in no uncertain terms their faith and belief in God the Creator. It is a mistake to think that science is essentially atheistic; it is radically the opposite.

The thoughtful reader at this point may inquire, "If this is true, why then are not all scientists Christians?" We believe that the answer is, "Because of faulty technique." Much of our recently acquired knowledge depends, of course, upon a machine technology, but the balance comes to us from the proper application of technique and the clarity of conclusion. As an example of what we mean, we might cite the very simple technique of research in protozoology.

When we find water that we suspect contains certain interesting forms of life, there is a recognized procedure that must be followed. This water is centrifuged to cast all the living matter into the bottom of a test tube, and the surplus water is drained off with a pipette. There is added to this small amount in the bottom of the test tube a few more centimeters of water impregnated with Eosin Y. This mild but persistent tissue stain will impregnate the entire morphology of any creature living in that water.

After a few hours have lapsed, to allow for this penetration, the specimen is again centrifuged and repeatedly rinsed in clear water. After the final centrifuging, we then have two or three centimeters of water in the bottom of the test tube containing an abnormal amount of living matter which is invisible to the unaided eye.

Now we draw out one drop of that water and place it on the concave surface of a glass slide. Over this cavity a cover glass is cemented into place and the finished slide is fitted to the mechanical stage of a compound microscope. The eyes of the observer approach the ocular lenses of this almost miraculous instrument, and magnified some two thousand times, this drop of water is turned into a miniature lake. In that clear background we see pink creatures speeding about on the ordinary business of their daily living, unveiling their secrets to the eye of the delighted beholder, and thus we learn the nature of the life resident in that water.

In other words, the technique of observation in protozoology is to observe the specimen through the microscope. Suppose, now, that the student had an improper technique. Let us say that his procedure was accurate up until the time he prepared the drop of water for observation on the glass slide. But supposing the scientist now took his glass slide in his hand, and going to the laboratory bench, he laid down the microscope and peered at the instrument through the specimen! How long would it take a skilled observer to find out the nature of life in the water, as long as he studied the instrument through the specimen?

At once you smile and say, "Nobody would be so foolish," from which conclusion we must reluctantly dissent.

The universe in which we live is our specimen. The Bible is our microscope. When men study creation through the lens of the Word of God, their definitions are clear, their enlargements are magnificent, and their conclusions are scientific and accurate. But when a man uses the universe, which is his specimen, to study the Word of God, which is his magnifying glass, he has reversed the proper procedure! So his definitions are fogged, the matter is distorted, and confusion results!

No scientist can see clearly and think straight, unless he first sees God; and then sees the universe through Him. Thus the difference between the scientist who is a Christian and one who is not, is a matter of methods and not materials. The scientist who looks at the physical universe through the Bible sees all matter in its proper relationship to spiritual verities, but the man who seeks to look at the Bible through the physical world has a fogged and befuddled vision and is confused.

We cannot emphasize this too strongly. It is a matter of method. If the telescope is reversed and the wrong end is placed to the eye, distant objects are indefinable and even the closest and most familiar things are warped and twisted out of their proper perspective.

There are two revelations of God in the world, and it is imperative that we keep these revelations in their proper relationship to each other. The lowest and simplest revelation that God has made of Himself is in the physical world that men call nature. But the natural testimony of the existence of God is unavailable to the general world of men. They must have a higher and clearer setting forth of His Person than that.

Because the *natural* revelation was not sufficient to lead men to God, He was forced to give them a *supernatural* revelation. In witness of the truth of this fact, we present the nations called "heathen". Abominable practices abound and incest abhorrent to the civilized world is common among them. Their lecherous conduct is frowned upon by every Christian nation. The manner of their hourly living can only be adequately termed "ungodly". Their vicious and vile practices, which are the common custom of their general living, condemn them to a bestial level.

Yet the heathen are in possession of nature as we are not! They dwell in the palm of nature's hand. They recline upon her bosom in the watches of the night, and they wring their sustenance by travail and daring from her reluctant grasp. The same seasons pass over them that we experience, the same sun warms them by day, and the same stars light their way by night, and yet they have no true knowledge of God.

It is thus evident that the natural revelation of God is inadequate fully to set Him forth. Hence God has given to men a higher revelation of Himself, in the pages of the Book called the Bible. It is the written revelation that came to men by the direct inspiration of the Holy Ghost, that deserves the highest place in the thinking of men today.

There are sermons in stones and homilies in the babbling brooks, to those who have seen God from some higher source of revelation! The very rocks *do* cry out to those who have found God through the higher medium of His Book. It is because of this incontestable fact, that science is the handmaid of Scripture. The two must ever be in perfect harmony, *where science is correct* and is truly scientific and not purely theoretical. So evident was this in the thinking of the eminent Sajous, that this great man of science cried out in delighted interest, "Science is doing even more for religious thought today; *it is acting as a beacon for the great pathway to God, which is the Bible!*"

Hand in hand they go about their work for the sons of men:

THE WORKS OF GOD
and
THE WORDS OF GOD

in perfect harmony and accord. The physical creation and the spiritual revelation breathe the same message that the Living Word journeyed from heaven to establish, which is, "The earth shall be filled with the knowledge of God as the waters cover the sea."

The Harmony of Science and Scripture

CHAPTER II

The Harmony of Science and the Scriptures

THE arguments offered in this pamphlet are but the acknowledged opinion of most of the thoughtful students of both science and the Bible. We do find in nature *a* revelation of God, even as we find in the Bible *the* revelation of Him. The only point of difference that now exists between the schools of philosophical opinions has to do with the matter of the harmony of these two revelations. Many men who have the power to read the signature of Deity in the works that He has wrought, do not go sufficiently into the problem of inspiration to make a complete harmony of fact and record. Therefore it is not uncommon to hear certain men who are not without standing in the scholarly world maintain that the Bible and science contradict each other. Those who concede the existence of contradictions between science and Scripture accept science as the more authoritative of the two, and are quick to charge error to the writers of the Bible.

This attitude of mind necessarily manifests no small egotism on the part of the objector. The budding knowledge of man in the world of science makes no claim to infallibility, so the controversy is really over the credibility of the two authorities. The true student is one who approaches the problem of alleged errors and contradictions in his field of correlation in a humble attitude of mind. Perhaps the mistake is not made by the writers of the Scripture. It may be simply an error in our understanding.

How often in recent months have we read of some marvelous discovery of science that was announced in screaming headlines in the morning of excitement, which was alleged to refute the old things of the Christian faith! Later in the day of investigation, however, when calm reason had had an opportunity to survey the alleged bases of such discoveries, doubt was cast upon the credibility of the first announcement. Finally, when the evening edition of that same widely advertised discovery was presented in cold, scientific terms, divorced from the hysteria of newspaper announcement, we found that the earlier conclusions were not predicated upon truth, and so fact had become disguised under fancy!

Some time ago we heard an eminent theologian apologize for the Bible, saying, "Of course there are scientific errors in the Bible. However, we can excuse such mistakes on the ground that the Bible is not a textbook of science, and therefore we do not expect it to be scientifically accurate."

The premise of this learned gentleman is a sound one, but his conclusion is utterly indefensible. Certainly the Bible is not a textbook of science. We are happy to agree with that premise. If the Bible were a textbook of science, it would have to be rewritten at least once in every generation. A textbook of science ten years of age is obsolete. The findings of one generation are subject to the broader research of the following generation, and scientific knowledge is in a constant state of flux. So when we have a book which has remained unchanged for multiplied centuries and which still retains its grip upon the heart and intelligence of the entire human family who are familiar with its contents, we recognize that we are not dealing with so temporary and fallible a work as would be a textbook of science.

Dr. R. A. Millikan, director of the Norman Bridges Laboratory of the California Institute of Technology, formulated the following statement: "The purpose of science is to develop, without prejudice or preconception of any kind, a knowledge of the facts, the laws, and the processes of nature. *The even more important task of religion,* on the other hand, is to develop the consciences, the ideals, and the aspirations of mankind."

How few textbooks of science are composed entirely of facts, written without prejudice or preconception of any kind! How few of the laws and processes of nature have been absolutely mastered in their entirety by the inquiring mind of man!

The Bible, however, not evolving from the

gradual accumulation of human wisdom, but being an involution of the mind of God into the thinking of men, is free from this constant correction and change. Regardless of the *purpose* of the Bible, it is the Word of God. This being so, errors of any kind would be inexcusable. In a book that owed its origin and authority to the perfect knowledge of Deity, no error of any kind could be admissible. Regardless of the reason for the writing, Almighty God knew the facts in all cases. Therefore, if errors of science are found in the Bible, its claims to inspiration are proved false and its divine authority has been disproved.

We would hasten to remind the reader, however, that only a science that is free from error will agree with a true and accurate rendition of the text of the Bible. Years ago the Research Science Bureau offered the sum of one hundred dollars to anyone who could demonstrate an unquestioned contradiction between a fact of science and a statement of the Scripture. Into our files there poured an amazing number of queries and applications from those who fancied that they had found a scientific mistake in the old Book. Upon analysis, however, every one of these so-called mistakes of the Bible turned out to be based upon the ignorance of the contender.

As an illustration, we would cite the communication of a young lady in Detroit, who is a graduate of the University of Michigan. This young lady wrote, saying that she would take the one hundred dollars offered for the proof of a scientific mistake in Holy Writ, and cited the following data: "It is inferred in the Scripture that the garden of Eden was in the land of Mesopotamia. Science has recently demonstrated that apples will not grow in the climate of Mesopotamia. But the Bible states that Adam and Eve were put out of the garden of Eden for eating an apple, in a climate where science has now proved that apples will not grow!" On this basis she demanded the one hundred dollars.

The committee replied to her very simply by asking for the citation in Scripture that stated that the fruit of Adam's misdemeanor was an apple. Of course, the Bible nowhere uses the word, "apple", in connection with Adam's fall. The text in Genesis simply says, "fruit", and there are many varieties of fruit that grow in Mesopotamia.

The young lady replied, after considerable lapse of time, by saying, "I cannot find the verse in Genesis that says it was an apple, but I am positive it was an apple, because my Sunday school teacher told me so!" This scientific society, however, is not paying one hundred dollars for what some Sunday school teacher may or may not think about the text of the Scripture. Their proposition is clear, simple, sincere, and explicit. Wherever there is a clear statement of fact in the Scripture, the ultimate conclusions of science will demonstrate that fact beyond any shadow of a doubt.

Some years ago, the late Dr. E. E. Slosson, one of the outstanding men of science in our generation, wrote an interesting little book entitled, "The Sermons of a Chemist." In the foreword to his book, Dr. Slosson said, "Science is moulting, and right now it looks funny. But I wish that we could get the world to realize that this changing phase of science is an evidence of growth and not decay."

That is a thought-provoking statement, perfectly expressed. Some time later, when we shared a platform with Dr. Slosson, we called his attention to this sentence from the introduction to his interesting book. He smiled when his memory stirred, and said, "I still feel that way." We said, "Dr. Slosson, that statement covers the case perfectly. Science *is* growing, but we would like to reply to you, sir, in the language of the hill-billy of the South, 'Science may be growing, but the Bible is done growed'!"

This erudite man of science looked up with quick interest and said, "Meaning what?"

"Meaning," we replied, "that for a growing science to criticize a fully grown revelation would have something of the audacity of a seven-year-old boy telling a seventy-year-old man how to grow up. It just isn't done that way, you know!"

By every technique that is acceptable, we test the lesser by the greater. This modern craze to test Scripture by science, however, would reverse the natural order. When science is grown up and has achieved its majority, and has demonstrated its own infallibility, we may then be ready to test the Bible by science. At the present time this proceeding is wrong, and we should reverse the technique. We have come to that place in our thinking, after twenty-five years of research on this subject, where we are willing to admit that where science and the Bible are in utter harmony, that agreement establishes the certainty *of that science!*

We must not forget that there are errors in scientific thought. The opinions of scientists change so rapidly that it is reported that the library of the Louvre, in Paris, contains three and one-half miles of bookshelves, holding volumes of science that have become obsolete in fifty years!

The reader may recall that famous list of fifty-one scientific facts published by the French Academy of Science in 1861, all of which contradicted some statement of the Scripture. Those few score years have gone by, and not one word of the Bible has been changed. In those same few score years, the knowledge of science has so vastly increased that there is not a living man of science today who holds one of those fifty-one so-called facts that were at one time advanced in refutation of the inspiration of the Scripture.

We are sure that a careful review of the last three score years of scientific opinion would show that a fiercer battle has raged between schools of scientific interpretation than has ever existed between the diverse camps of varying denominational beliefs.

We feel confident that it should be easy to establish the harmony of science and Scripture. In four simple but clear propositions, we would summarize a great deal of evidence which, if given in detail, would fill many volumes the size of this one.

The first proposition is that the Bible *does* contain scientific truth even though its facts are stated in non-scientific language. Some time ago we heard of a very learned gentleman who repudiated the fact of the scientific accuracy of the Scripture. He based his entire attitude of mind upon the fact that the Bible does not contain the language of science. Therefore he concluded that the Book could not be scientifically reliable.

Of course, we are quick to admit the fact that the Bible does not contain the language of science, and we are very glad that this is so. For the expression of human thought, language is a vehicle which is invented and changed to meet the needs of every passing generation. The language of modern science is as modern as science is recent. Its appearance in a Book from two to four thousand years of age would constitute so glaring an evidence of anachronism as to rob that Book of any authority or value whatever.

If we picked up a purportedly ancient volume which was supposed to have been written in the fifteenth century, and we found therein references to such modern mechanical parts as carburetor, magneto, differential, transmission, et cetera, we would cast the book aside with a laugh, knowing that it could not have been written at the time it was supposed to have been. This illustration is exact in application to this objection. The language of science was produced to meet the needs of a generation centuries after the writing of the Bible was completed.

Again, if the Bible were written in the peculiar vocabulary of modern science, it would be beyond the understanding and use of the common man. The language of science is not only wonderful, it is sometimes weird. Although laymen have had a great deal of enjoyment poking fun at the multisyllabic vocabulary of men of science, there is of course, a practical and reasonable basis for all the technical expressions.

We remember some years ago sitting around a campfire where we were engaged in excavating relics of more or less antiquity from the burial heaps where they had slumbered for centuries. In the course of the evening's relaxation, a young medico who was one of the party introduced an ingenious game. He gave to each contestant a line from the famous, familar old nursery song, "There was an old nigger, and his name was Ned, and he died long, long ago." The rule of the game demanded that each man should reduce the line in his possession to the best scientific language at his command.

The man who won the prize had for his sentence, "He had no hair on the top of his head in the place where the hair ought to grow."

When this ingenious young fellow had finished his sentence in the finest scientific diction, it read as follows: "He possessed no follicle appendages on the cutaneous apex of his cranial structure, anterior to the sagittal suture and posterior to the lambdoidal suture, where said follicle appendages habitually germinate."

Now, what a way to say that the man was bald! Would the reader seriously consider studying a Bible that was written in language like that? The illustration may sound ridiculous, but it serves to show the folly of such criticism directed against the Scripture.

Certainly the Bible does not contain the language of science, but *it does contain* scientific fact. This absence of technical language, however, has no reverse bearing on the question of inspiration. It takes an unusual type of wisdom and ability to be able to express the deep and marvelous things of science in language so simple that a child can read and comprehend. As long as scientific fact may clearly be discerned in the Bible, it matters not in what sort of language those expressions of fact may be couched. And that the Bible does contain the facts of science, will be clearly demonstrated to the satisfaction of the honest and intelligent reader before this volume is completed.

The second, and even more important, line of evidence, may be shown by the fact that the Bible does not contain the errors and fallacies of science common to the age of its production. We are all more or less familiar with the now refuted argument of the modernist, that the Bible is simply the result of varying types of culture. We are told that certain writers of the Scripture lived in successive stages of culture. Moses, for instance, lived under an Egyptian culture. Some of the later prophets lived under a Persian culture, some under a Babylonian culture, and some under a Chaldean culture. The argument of modernism has been that these various writers incorporated into their section of the Scripture the accepted wisdom of the age in which they lived. Because the things they wrote happened to be true, their books have survived down through the ages.

This is a fascinating theory, but it has two things wrong with it. The first thing is, it is not true. The second thing is, there is no semblance of veracity in the entire theory!

Surely there were men who lived under varying cultures, but they did not write the wisdom of their day in the books that bear their name. Moses, for instance, "was learned in all the wisdom of the Egyptians." This man Moses was reared as the crown prince of Egypt. Being adopted by the daughter of Pharaoh, he became the heir apparent to the throne. The finest education that Egyptian wisdom could provide was his. Being endowed by God with an unusually brilliant mentality, re-enforced by a strong personality, he became one of the leaders of his generation.

Commentators seem to have lost sight of the fact that when Moses answered the call of God and offered himself as the emancipator of his enslaved brethren, he surrendered the sceptre of a kingdom that was practically a universal dominion; counting it better to suffer for a time with the people of God and to reign with them in an eternal kingdom forever. So Moses, educated in the finest schools of Egypt, *was* "learned in all the wisdom of the Egyptians".

However, in this generation we can boast of that same wisdom and learning which Moses possessed. Through the marvelous discoveries of the science of archaeology, we can read those same texts that Moses and the men of his generation studied in the schools of Egypt in that day. Their "wisdom" was weird, utterly unbased upon fact, and consisted of some of the wildest, most impossible imaginings that the earth has ever known.

The ancient Egyptians, for instance, believed that the earth had hatched from a winged egg, which flew around in space until the process of mitosis was completed and the earth emerged from that flying ovoid. Now, remember that Moses was learned in all the wisdom of the Egyptians. This constituted their science of geology. The very opening chapter of the Mosaic sections of the Old Testament begin with a statement of geology and the systematic cosmogony that accompanies his presentation of this science. The modernistic theory has been that Moses wrote what he learned in the schools of Egypt.

There is an element of humor in that very contention, when we remember that just a few years ago the modernists were asserting with dogmatic assurance that writing was not invented until five hundred years after the age of Moses. Now calmly, and with equal assurance, they reverse themselves and say that he wrote just what he learned in the schools of that day.

So, then, we turn to the writings of Moses to read about this winged egg. We are somewhat surprised, in the face of this theory of criticism, to find that it is never mentioned from the beginning of his cosmogony to the end thereof. In the place of this weird claptrap of ancient ignorance, we find the ten most comprehensive words that were ever put together in human speech: "In the beginning God created the heaven and *the earth.*" With that dictum of Moses, which utterly repudiated the wisdom accepted in his generation, modern science has not been able to prove or demonstrate one point of difference.

The Egyptians also had a science of anthropology. This is the science of man, and the Egyptians were naive evolutionists. They taught that men originally hatched from certain white worms that were found in the slime of the Nile after the annual deluge. We presume that they had witnessed the metamorphosis of the caterpillar into the moth or the butterfly, and predicated their evolutionary hypothesis upon that observed phenomenon.

This, of course, is the technique of the modern evolutionary school. It also observes one scientific fact which is conceded by all schools of thought, and upon that single grain of sand it erects a mountain range of supposition. If the theory of evolution *were* true, then we would prefer the Egyptian idea! Far better to have nice, clean fishbait for ancestry than flea-bitten apes in some primeval jungle!

Be that as it may, our point still remains, that Moses "was learned in all the wisdom of the Egyptians."

So when he picked up his pen to write of the origin of man, he told of their metamorphosis from worms into human beings, did he not?

Yes, he did not!

In majestic language, which has never been surpassed by human pen from that hour to this, Moses wrote of an infinite God stooping to a finite sphere to form a body for man with His own hands. Into this body the Omnipotent Creator breathed the breath of life, and man became a living soul. Once more we state that the conclusions of Mosaic anthropology have never been successfully refuted by any school of science in the last four thousand years. As we have done with these two sciences, by way of illustration, so we might do with all the sciences taught in the schools of Egypt when Moses walked the earth.

As far as astronomy is concerned, the Egyptian masters taught that the sun reflected the light of the earth. Moses, however, reversed their scholarly conclusions and brought his cosmogony into absolute agreement with the demonstrated facts of science as they have been derived from our modern knowledge of the solar system.

It is true, of course, that there were prophets who lived under a Chaldean culture. It is equally true that they never in one single instance introduced that culture into their writings. The Chaldeans, at one stage of their culture, believed that the earth was a living creature. They taught that this live, sleeping monster had covered himself with feathers and scales in the form of vegetation and rocks. They believed that men were but vermin which lived on the skin of this sleeping monster, as fleas live on the hide of a dog. Not a very exalted idea, but at least that is what they believed! They taught that if one dug deeply enough into the skin of this monster to hurt him, he would shake himself, and the buildings would fall down! Men *did* dig into the earth in their search for precious metals, and earthquakes *did* occur and buildings *were* shaken down. This constituted, to them, satisfactory scientific proof of the accuracy of their theories.

We admit, again, that there were prophets who wrote under this culture. Will the reader kindly point out the place in the Scripture where this Chaldean nonsense was incorporated into the writings of those prophets? If a reader can produce any such instance, the author of this volume stands ready to pay a thousand dollars for the citation and the accompanying proof. We frankly admit that we do not have a thousand dollars, but we are also fairly convinced that we will have millions before such a case can be discovered!

Surely there were writers who lived under a Babylonian culture, Daniel being perhaps the most famous of them all. Daniel, however, did not learn from the wisdom of Babylon, but the wisest of Babylon learned from Daniel. Kings and conquerors hung upon his words and obeyed his slightest suggestion. One of the greatest books of the Bible came from the pen of this man Daniel, who is supposed, according to the critical theory, to have written only the wisdom common to his age.

The reader may recall one of the many creation legends of Babylon, that tells of the battle fought between the chaos monster, Tiamat, and the great god Marduke. This battle ended when Marduke was victorious and slew Tiamat. Not wishing to waste the great body, Marduke rolled the carcass of Tiamat up, fastened it with its own tail, and stepped on it, squashing it out flat. We then learn how the god, Marduke, began spitting; and wherever he spat, men sprang into being, full grown and erect. The men, in turn, began spitting, and where they spat, women suddenly emerged from the sod like the soldiers who came from the dragon's teeth which were sowed by Jason. When there were women enough for all the men, they ceased this unique method of creation, and the women began spitting. Where they spat, animals sprang into being, and thus the earth was created and populated!

What utter and ridiculous nonsense it is even to consider that this Babylonian science could find a place in the Book that tells men of the existence of God and of His mercy and grace! If, then, a Book was produced over a period of two thousand years, and every scientific fallacy of those two millennia was religiously excluded from its pages, a wisdom more than human is manifested therein. Not only did the Spirit of God reveal that which was true to the writers, but it becomes increasingly apparent that He also ruled out everything that was untrue. By this forethought and wisdom of an omniscient Author, the Bible was kept in harmony with the discoveries of our generation, that we might find it acceptable in the day when a truly modern science unfolded to us some of the secrets of the universe.

The third reason for saying that the Bible is in harmony with modern science is the remarkable fashion in which the Bible disagrees with modern error, exactly as it has contradicted ancient fallacy. This, indeed, is the source of the present controversy. There are certain men, wise above that which is written, who are enamored of their own super-learning. They never hesitate to state probabilities and theories in the dogmatic terms of certainties. Their *conclusions* (which may, indeed be *based* upon fact) are to be received as infallible, or else their dignity suffers. When men of this type come face to face with the teachings of the Scripture, their mental attitude is, "Away with such a Book, that dares to contradict us!"

Every student who has gone through a full college and university course has met this attitude repeatedly, if he attended a typical institution of higher learning. The Bible is declared to be old-fashioned, out-moded, fallible, unscientific, and teeming with error, merely because it does not agree with the theories and conclusions of fallible men. There have been men in other generations who have also thought that the Bible should have been re-written to conform to their conclusions. Had the men of that generation, however, tampered with the sacred Word of God to bring it into harmony with what they fondly believed to be undisputed fact, the Bible today would be useless to our generation. In that same manner, if we did re-write the Bible today to suit the learned professors in those same institutions, within twenty-five years the world would be laughing at the Bible which we had re-written.

Most of the controversy, of course, has come from the single field that deals with the problems of origin. We may as well state at the very outset that it is crass nonsense to talk about a *science* of origin. In science we deal not with origin. That is rather the sphere of philosophy. Philosophy, in turn, depends entirely upon human conclusions. Unless we are prepared to make the assertion that our generation has reached absolute perfection, we cannot well claim that our philosophies will not need to be revised by a coming generation.

To illustrate this thought with a practical question, we would suggest the utter incompatibility between the two present theories of the origin of man. The first of these theories is the Mosaic statement of specific creation. To this is opposed the philosophical theory called organic evolution. Between these two theories every thoughtful student must make his choice. We have, of course, heard of those who maintain that they could and did believe in both evolution and creation. This school generally denominates itself as "believers in theistic evolution".

The fact of the matter, however, is that these two theories are in such unquestioned opposition that one cannot believe the Bible to be the infallible Word of God and hold to the theory of organic evolution. We have seen men who could ride two horses at the same time. This is a common spectacle in the circus, and is often seen in the western rodeos, when the cowboys are at play. When the cavalry of any army are putting on their field-days, this is one of their most thrilling spectacles. We have noticed, however, that when a man rides two horses at the same time, *he is careful to keep them close together and both going in the same direction!*

We never saw a rider so skillful that he could ride two horses at the same time when they were headed in opposite directions!

This, then, is the weakness of the theistic evolutionary school of philosophy. The Bible gives a plain, simple account of the creation of man, in terms that a child can understand. By a fiat act, possible only to Omnipotence, Almighty God created man by a miraculous process.

The word for this creation that is used in the text of the Hebrew Old Testament is "bara". Every commentary and lexicon that deals with the text of the Old Testament is careful to note that the word "bara" means "to form something out of nothing", or "to call into existence that which had no previous form or substance." The Mosaic account of creation states that man was made perfect, in the image and likeness of God. From this high position as God's fellow, man fell to a depth of sin and degradation lower than the moral condition of the beasts of the field. From that low position he never climbed by his own power, intellect, wisdom, or spirit. Indeed, to that fallen estate he would have been condemned forever, had it not been that Jesus Christ came and lifted him.

In a word, then, the theory of creation starts man as high as he can possibly be and portrays his fall to the lowest depths.

Opposed to all this is the theory of organic evolution. According to this school of philosophy, man began as an infinitely small microscopic mass of protoplasmic substance, too low and humble and small even to be visible to the unaided powers of the human eye. From this lowly estate, by an infinite number of gradual changes, man has climbed, unaided by any external force, until he is today the highest living thing in the realm of biology.

Here, then, are two opposing theories.

One says that man was created perfect and fell.

The other says that man *happened* to start, and if he ever fell, he fell *up* in his age-long climb.

Of course, we understand why certain educators and men who are filled with the pride of the flesh would reject the Genesis account of creation. It must be clear to the reader who thinks this through that if the story of creation is true, the story of a fall into sin is equally so. If we accept the fact of the fall into sin, we must also accept the certainty of our own guilt and iniquity. If this is accepted, in turn there remains no possibility of escape, save that which is offered in the Scriptures.

The single means of redemption from the effect of the fall is to humble ourselves before the cross of Calvary and cleanse ourselves in the blood that was shed thereon.

This is the one thing that the proud and stubborn hearts of self-satisfied men will not do. So in order to escape the necessity of the confession of sin and the humble suit for pardon in Jesus' Name, they deny the foundational fact and seek to change the predication. But when the tumult and the shouting have died, and the captains of science and the kings of education have departed to their long and final resting-place, the world will come again to a truly scientific investigation of the evidences of the origin of man. The Word of God will emerge triumphant in that hour, because it has courageously opposed the false theories of a mistaken philosophy.

We would advance a fourth and final reason for saying that the Bible is in harmony with modern science. That reason may be stated in this brief phrase: The Bible is in harmony with modern science, in that it has anticipated many of the discoveries of these recent centuries.

We remember some time ago that a very excited and dogmatic correspondent wrote to tell us of a ridiculous scientific error that Isaiah had made in his prophecy. This correspondent stated that Isaiah had made the assertion that the earth was flat, whereas modern science has proved that it is round. We wrote to the correspondent and asked for a citation, for we are not familiar with any reference in Isaiah that states that the earth is flat. This man wrote at some length and said the assertion was made in Isaiah 11:12. Of course, we were familiar with this verse, as it is one of the stock quotations of every infidel and critical rejecter of the Scripture.

Quoting the verse from Isaiah, "And he shall set up an ensign for the nations, and shall assemble the outcasts of Israel, and gather together the dispersed of Judah from the four corners of the earth", our correspondent triumphantly stated that if Isaiah said the earth had four corners, he must have believed it was flat. He then followed with this question: "Would you trust yourself on board a ship whose captain believed that the earth had four corners?"

This query caused the writer considerable amusement, as we had just returned from an ocean voyage of several thousand miles, sailing on one of the great liners that plied the Pacific. The captain of that vessel was not only a friend of the writer, but one of the most genial companions it is possible to have while sailing the deep. In the course of a heavy blow that tossed the ship about and played with it as a terrier would worry a rat, we made some reference to the storm. This reference evoked considerable amusement on the part of the captain, who laughed and said, "This is not a storm; this is just a good stiff breeze!"

When we expressed some skepticism concerning his knowledge of storms, the captain waxed warm and said, "I have been in the four corners of the earth, and I have seen a storm in every one of them; this is only a strong blow." We dropped the argument, as we had only sought to stir up the captain to some such statement, hoping to get some reminiscence from him, which was always a delightful experience. But when this correspondent indignantly protested Isaiah's language, we could not help remembering the captain who thought he had been to the four corners of the earth, and was thus as ignorant as Isaiah!

Also, some time ago we received a brochure from the United States government, advertising the work of the U.S. Marine Corps. One sentence in that leaflet sticks in our mind, "The United States marines are serving the flag today at the four corners of the earth." Now what do you think of that? The United States government thinks the earth is flat, and that it has a marine with a flag standing on each one of its four corners! Of course, that's nonsense.

The phrase, "the four corners of the earth" is a poetic expression meaning exactly the same as the expression, "the four points of the compass." It must be remembered that Isaiah was also a poet, and if he desired to speak in poetic language, he had a poet's license so to do. If Isaiah *had* said, "the four corners of the earth", he would have had no more intent to define the shape of the earth than did this writer of the United States government staff.

The fact of the matter, however, is that Isaiah never said, "the four corners of the earth." That is an English phrase, and Isaiah neither spoke nor wrote the English language. Isaiah wrote in Hebrew, and when we read his text in the Hebrew, he literally said that "God would gather together the dispersed of Judah from the *four quarters* of the earth". It is an accepted fact that any round object can be cut into quarters. (We know that to be so, as we had two sisters and a brother. We have seen many an apple cut into four quarters, and oranges likewise!)

While every infidel knows this English mistranslation of the words of Isaiah, we have never found one of them honest enough to refer to the only text in the book of Isaiah where the prophet *did* speak about the shape of the earth. This is in Isaiah 40:22, where the prophet writes concerning the greatness and the magnitude of God, "It is he that sitteth *above the circle* of the earth." Again, we must note that the word, "circle", is a translation of a Hebrew word that literally means "roundness". The most literal translation from the Hebrew into a vernacular text that we have ever found on this point is that of the modern Swedish translation. In place of the word "circle", the Swedish version uses the word "rund", which is a literal rendition of the idea of Isaiah.

There were doubtless those of Isaiah's generation who believed the earth to be flat. There have been some in every generation, including the present, who have held this erroneous idea. The point that we desire to stress, however, is that when Isaiah wrote, he was not limited by the extent of his own learning. When the Spirit of God guided his pen, he wrote by inspiration, setting down for our learning things that men had not yet discerned in his day. A great many centuries went by, nay, even thousands of years, before men established the fact that the earth was round.

But when by their search and study, their adventure and investigation, men learned this fact, lo, the Bible had anticipated their discovery ages before! By this unique and remarkable method of anticipating the scientific discoveries of coming centuries, the Spirit of God kept the Word of His truth in harmony with modern science.

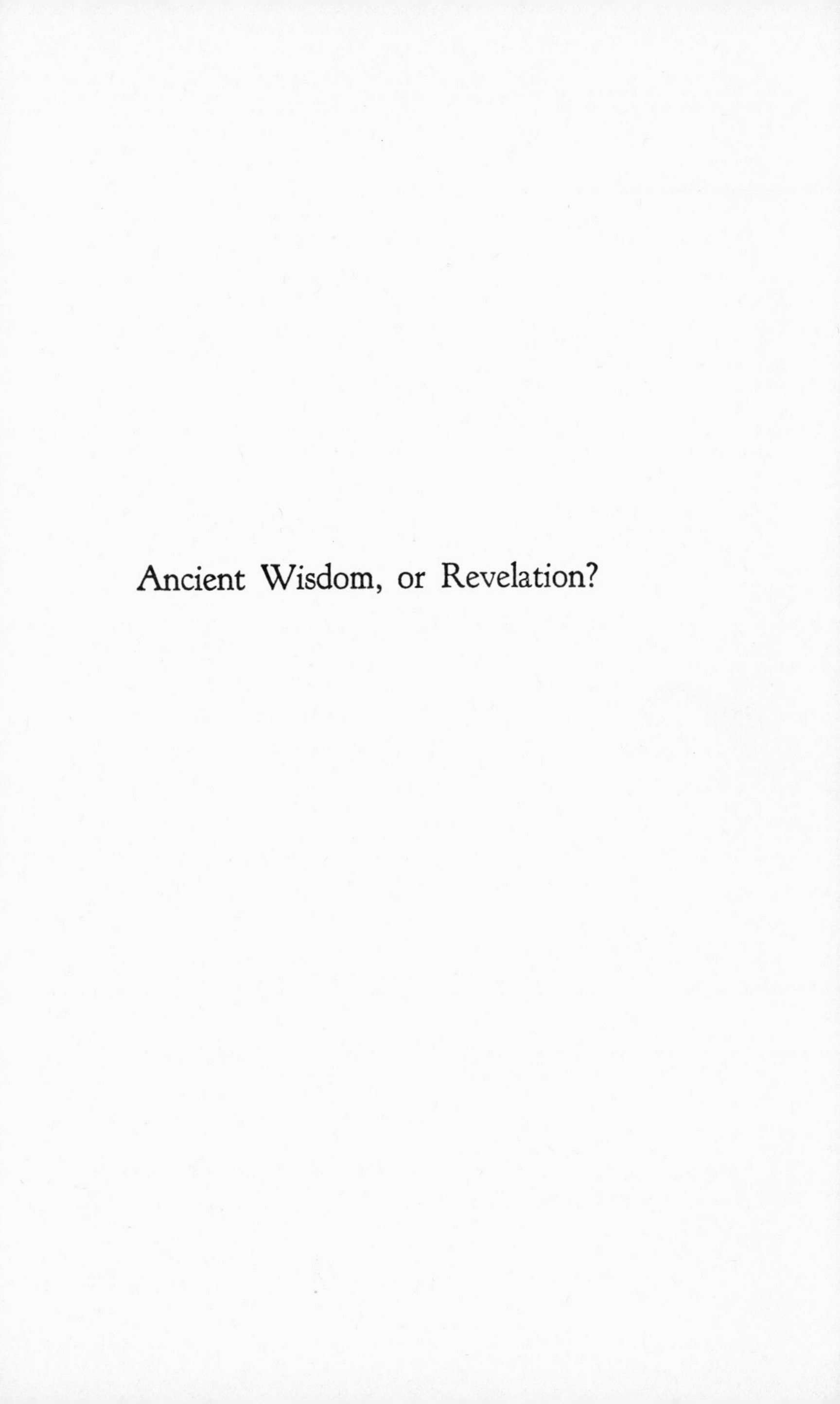

Ancient Wisdom, or Revelation?

CHAPTER III

Ancient Wisdom, or Revelation?

IT WOULD be folly for any intelligent human being to question the marvelous progress of this age. We are surrounded on every hand by indisputable evidences of the mechanical ingenuity of our generation, which is our modern criterion of an advancing culture. With an engaging lack of false modesty, man named himself the genus homo sapiens. There is only one genus of man, and but one species. There are several varieties of homo sapiens, and it seems as though if one desired to become slightly humorous, one might suggest that it were time to rename our modern variety of man. No longer should he be denominated as sapient. It is time now to classify this generation as the "genus homo *scientifaciens.*"

We realize, of course, that if one is not scientific now, one just is not! Perhaps the best way to get a picture of the cultural progress of our generation would be to contrast the culture of the twentieth century A. D. with that of the twentieth century B. C. In almost every avenue and channel of living, we have made wonderful progress. In the case of transportation alone, we could surely prove our contention that we are far ahead of our primitive ancestors.

In those ancient days when one was in a hurry to journey, his swiftest means of travel was the horse. If the horse didn't balk, run out of hay, or decide to turn away from the path and go his own sweet course, man could flee across the terrain at the astounding speed of fifty miles a day. But in our generation when we desire to get somewhere else in a hurry, we climb into a vehicle to which we have given the wings of a dove, and cross continents and oceans at a speed of two hundred and fifty miles an hour. Verily, indeed, has the genius of this generation conquered the realms of space.

Or even more startling is the progress in the field of communication. Our minds go back in fancy to the time when some ancient business man entered his innermost office cave and saluted his stenographer with these words, "Miss Stonehatchet, take a letter." In our fancy we see two strong men carrying in a stone block, while the maiden grabs her chisel in one hand and her hammer in the other and prepares to take dictation. It might have been amusing, had we been a spectator, to see the stenographer get angry at her boss and begin to throw carbon copies about the office!

But now in this ingenious generation when one is in a hurry to communicate, he dictates to a machine. There are offices in our land that are connected with as many as thirty far distant cities, by a marvelous mechanism called the teletype. The head of one of these concerns, desiring to communicate with all of his branch managers, speaks to the operator of this machine, whose flying fingers depress keys as fast as the speaker can dictate. Instantly, without any appreciable lapse of time, in a score and a half far-flung cities, machines synchronize to the one in the home office and reproduce the words of the executive as fast as they can fall from his lips. A hundred miles, a thousand miles, or three thousand miles, make no difference in communication today.

Very often the writer has taken down the phone in New York City and saluted the operator with the number of his home in distant Los Angeles. Fifteen seconds after the operator has received the call, a loved one in Los Angeles is speaking into our ear. Recognizing the voice, we say, "Hello," and although we are separated by three thousand miles of space, the answer is instantaneous. No lapse of time of any longer duration than that required by light to make that same journey, ensues before the reply falls upon our listening ear. This, to a past generation, would have appeared miraculous. We hasten to remark that we do not mean that it is unusual that a man's wife answers back instantly. Rather, we seek to convey the impression that an answer fleeing across three thousand miles of space and arriving in the very span of time that the breath of the speaker passes her lips, would strain the credulity of the ancients.

In the reproduction of the written word, with automatic presses grinding out hundreds of thousands of words a minute, which words are distributed over counties and states ere the ink is dry upon the paper, mark the progress of humanity in the conquest of culture. Verily was Job premature when he said to the men of his generation, "No doubt ye are the people, and wisdom will perish with you." We are almost convinced that if Job had waited until our generation, he could have made his famous sarcastic fling and it would have been received as solemn truth by us to whom it was later addressed.

Yet when all this has been said and done, there is in the dim recesses of our conscience a monitor which seeks to call attention to what we are pleased to call "lost arts".

When men talk about perfection in architecture, their minds journey back to ancient Karnak or to the Coliseum, whose ruins astound the tourist today.

When men speak of sculpture, they breathe with awe the name of Phidias.

In the realm of painting, voices hushed with reverence comment upon the work of the *old* masters, and in some things we have made progress backwards.

The chief sphere in which man must stand humbly before the mystery of antiquity is in the realm of literature. Almost two thousand years ago, the pen of the last writer of the great Book was laid aside, and no word has been added to the Bible in the long succession of hurrying centuries. Yet the wisest of men on the earth still go to this great Book of vast antiquity for the highest inspiration that literature contains.

One of the greatest wonders of the Scripture is the manner in which its writers have anticipated much of our modern scientific discovery. This thesis cannot be disregarded when an honest inquirer seeks to survey the problem of the harmony of science and Scripture. Remembering that the Bible was written multiplied centuries before our modern knowledge was gathered, it is inconceivable that human wisdom could have kept that book in harmony with our advancing discoveries. So when, in the laboratory of science, we make some marvelous discovery in our generation and then find that the writers of the Bible had incorporated our discovery in their ancient records, we find ourselves between the horns of a dilemma.

Shall we decide that the ancients were in possession of our modern scientific knowledge? We could not concede that possibility.

First, our body of knowledge and wisdom, slowly accumulating by painstaking accretion over hundreds of years, is indeed far in advance of that possessed in those dim, dark years when the Bible was being written. Undoubtedly, the heritage of the recent years upon which we have builded our modern structure of super-learning, has come by painstaking investigation, all of which has been demonstrated by experimentation. We must not forget, also, that as Ayers has so truthfully pointed out, "Modern scientific discovery is the result of a machine technology." By that, Ayers meant to convey a picture not only of the technique but of the equipment of modern research and study.

What is the great advance in biology? You might say that it was the discovery of the apparatus Golgi that fluctuates in the cytoplasm of the cell. In that case, you would be wrong. The great discovery in biology is the invention of the super-microscope that makes apparatus Golgi visible to the human eye. When we have the instrument at our command, it is inevitable that we shall discover the things made visible by that instrument.

The great advance in physics is not the isolation of the atom, but is rather the invention of such instruments of research as the spectroscope and the super X-ray microscope, which make the atom ponderable to human understanding.

When men have the telescope, it is only logical that the solar system shall consequently dawn upon their vision and understanding.

Men could not know of the existence of the infinitely microscopic bacteria before the microscope revealed them to human vision. Since our modern advancement is dependent upon instruments of precision that were totally unknown to the ancients, it follows that by wisdom and understanding alone these men of old could not have possessed our current body of knowledge.

Therefore, if these men in antiquity did write in one Book things that we are learning today with our new machines of investigation, the only other explanation is that an Intelligence higher than human directed their writings, and their material was derived by revelation. So then, the greatest argument for the inspiration of the Bible and the surest proof of its harmony with science would be to find in the pages of this ancient Book instances wherein the writers anticipated the discoveries of modern science. *It is possible for the careful student of science and Scripture to discover literally scores of such anticipations!*

We would start, for instance, by citing the fact that in the first chapter of Genesis, Moses divided the workdays of God into six periods of time, consummating with the creation of man. The modern science of biology places vegetation at the bottom of the scale of life. Coming up through the water-dwelling creatures to the lower forms of the metazoa which dwell upon the land, the advancing scale of life climaxes with man. This arrangement of vital life in ascending orders, demanded by the science of biology, meets the acquiescence of Moses, who has placed the orders of creation in the exact systematic advancement that biologists contend for today. The only difference between Moses and biology is that biologists contend for a superhatching process by which one order evolved from the other, while Moses contends for the more scientific explanation of specific creation of each order in turn.

We are somewhat surprised to note that on the third of those creative days, in dealing with physical geography, Moses makes this simple statement: "And God said, Let all the waters under the heaven be gathered into one place, and let the dry land appear." The word that Moses used in the Hebrew is "maqom", and it should be literally translated, "one bed". The statement of Moses, then, is that in this act of creation God gathered all of the oceans together into one bed. We suggest that the reader take his globe of the earth and trace his finger from point to point, journeying from sea to sea. The reader will find that Moses was literally and scientifically accurate in this simple statement. All the waters under the heavens *are* gathered together into one place.

Moses was careful, however, to keep the oceans separated, in that he put them in the plural in the statement, "And God called the dry land earth, and the gathering together of the waters called he seas." In the day when Moses walked the earth, the one sea that was known to men was the Mediterranean, and perhaps some small regions of the nearby Atlantic. When the seven seas were discovered and became known to men, it was not long before all of their magnitude had been explored by the eager interest of humanity. Whereupon we find that Moses had apparently sailed their uncharted bosoms before our ships of discovery and search were builded and launched! We know now that the oceanography of Moses was accurate, in that the seven seas *do* occupy one bed. How did Moses know this? Had he discovered this fact by human wisdom and research? The casual reader will say, "That's just a coincidence." For the sake of that reader, we will admit that this could be a coincidence, and look again.

Our famous California scientist, Dr. Robert Millikan, some time ago received the Nobel prize in physics for isolating the atom and making it ponderable to human vision. Dr. Millikan, of course, did not discover the atom, nor invent the atomic theory. Men had been familiar with the theoretical existence of the atom for many years before Dr. Millikan consummated his great work. We can remember back in the days more than a score of years ago, when we attended college. We had a professor by the name of Dr. Brooks, whom the boys facetiously called, "Up and at 'em Brooks", for every time the good doctor got up, he was sure to talk about the atom. Indeed, a lad not prepared to recite sometimes escaped the threatened doom by getting the good doctor interested in a discussion of the atomic theory. In this manner we learned a great deal about the atom, all of which, we have since found out, was not so! But that is the general fate of a college education. You spend four years learning things to pass examinations. You spend the next twenty-four years finding out that what you learned was not necessarily true!

For instance, Dr. Brooks conveyed to us the dogmatic idea that the atom was the smallest divisible particle of matter that the human mind could conceive. He assured us that no eye would ever see the atom, as it was the ultimate division of matter, and man's ingenuity would never make it visible. He gave us the idea that atoms were little solid globes of matter like ball bearings or marbles or solid rubber balls.

While it is true that the atom is infinitely small, it is not the ultimate division of matter. We might offer as the best description of an atom the statement that it is a skin-full of nothing, with satellites of nothing revolving around a nucleus, — except that it has no skin! It has been stated that if all the space were squeezed out of the atoms of a two hundred pound man, enough solid material would be left to cover the head of an ordinary pin. The man who realizes this, is not apt to get angry when his wife accuses him of being full of hot air. He knows that she is also, and preserves a dignified silence!

Now it is found that even these tiny components of the atom, the proton, the neutron, the electron, and so forth, follow known mechanical laws and travel on prescribed orbits, exactly as do the satellites of a solar system. The infinite minuteness of the atom has been lost sight of in view of the comparatively enormous mass an atom is found to be, in comparison with its component parts.

All this, of course, is kindergarten science, and well known to the average reader. We merely cite this to call attention to the fact that the atomic theory was apparently first discovered by Paul the Apostle! The best statement of the atomic theory that literature contains is found in the eleventh chapter of Hebrews, in the third verse. In this magnificent record of the heroes of faith and the triumphs they wrought by its virtues, we find these words, "Through faith we understand that the worlds were framed by the Word of God, so that things which are seen are not made of things which do appear."

This translation into the English is, of course, from the original Greek of the New Testament. The particular word in the Greek is "aionas", and according to the well-remembered dissertation of Dean Alford, "aionas" includes the world itself and all things therein. The expression, "hoi aiones" includes in it all that exists under the conditions of time and space. Together with those conditions of time and space themselves, things which have actual being do not exist independently of God, but are themselves the work of His Word. The more recent work of the eminent James Hope Moulton bears out this conclusion and statement of the eminent Dean Alford, so that the translation of the English is as accurate in sense as it is possible for a translation to be.

To put this famed statement of Paul into a paraphrase of English, we would adjust the idiom to our vocabulary in this fashion, "By faith we understand that the worlds were builded by the Word of God, so that things which are visible are made of entities that are invisible." This is as clear a statement of the atomic theory as it is possible for the human pen to write. Dr. Millikan received the Nobel prize of almost two score thousand dollars for proving this theory. Paul the Apostle did not receive so much as a dime for anticipating the discoveries of Millikan by eighteen centuries!

The point that we now raise is, How did Paul the Apostle know of the atom those hundreds of years before men discovered it?

Again the casual reader would say, "This is a coincidence."

And once more we smile and pass on to another demonstration.

In the day when the prophet Job walked the face of the earth, all men believed that the earth had some kind of solid foundations. Many, varied, and ingenious are the tales that have come down to us from the ancients, accounting for the suspension of the earth in space. We are told that the Egyptians believed, for instance, that the earth was supported by five great pillars, one under each corner and one in the middle. In our youthful days when we studied mythology, *this* theory left us strangely cold. We could understand that, had the earth been flat and square, someone *might* have peered over the edge to view the corner pillars, but that one in the middle was pure postulation!

We have all heard the Greek legend of Atlas, who stood with his head bowed, bearing the earth on his neck and shoulders. Again, we remember our childish wonder as to what supported Atlas.

Indeed, the only myth from antiquity that seems at all satisfactory is the ancient Hindu legend, which states that the earth is balanced on the back of a gigantic elephant. This elephant, in turn, is standing on an immense turtle. The turtle is swimming in a cosmic sea. That is the most satisfactory theory of all! It gives something for everything else to rest upon!

But in that day when men were dreaming their weird explanations of how the earth was held in place, the prophet Job picked up his pen to write about the greatness and the wonder of God. In the course of his description of the might of the heavenly Father, he wrote, "He stretcheth out the horizon over the empty place and *hangeth the earth upon nothing.*"

The word that Job here used is "belimah", and it is not a Hebrew word. Lexicographers are not in full agreement as to its origin, but it is presumed to have been from the vocabulary of ancient Sumeria. The meaning is nebulous, and "nothing" is as close to its meaning as we can arrive at this late date.

Some time ago we were attending a convention of the American Association for the Advancement of Science. At one of the banquets, we found ourselves seated next to a fellow member of a certain section of the association, who had a nation-wide reputation as a physicist and geographer. In the course of the conversation we said to this distinguished savant, "Doctor, what is it that holds the earth in place?"

This noted educator replied, "It is gravity that holds the earth in place."

We said, "Thank you, doctor, and what is gravity?"

With a twinkle in his eye, this kindly gentleman said, "Gravity, my boy, is what holds the earth in place!"

Now isn't that clear? That's lovely; that's scientific and conclusive. What holds the earth in place? Gravity. What is gravity? That which holds the earth in place!

This great and learned scholar gave the same answer that Job did, "on nothing". The scientist, however, used a handful of words where Job used only one. Now put the modern nebulous term "gravity" in the place of "belimah", and hear this man saying some four thousand years ago, "God stretcheth out the horizon over an empty place, and He hangeth the earth upon gravity."

How did Job know this?

He didn't.

But he wrote it!

Yes, says the objector, but that is only a coincidence. All right, we will concede that this might be a coincidence, and press on to another illustration.

Centuries upon centuries before Christ was born, multiplying themselves into a thousand years, the writer of Ecclesiastes picked up his pen and wrote, "All the rivers run into the sea, and yet the sea is not full. Unto the place from whence the rivers come, thither they return again." Of course, many men have pondered this problem. All the rivers do run into the sea, yet the sea is not full. Have you ever thought that through?

Every year the continents and islands of this earth pour down into the ocean a stupendous volume of water.

Let the reader contemplate, for just a moment, a cubic mile of water. That would be a lake a mile long, a mile square, and a mile deep. The stupendous weight of a cubic mile of water would stagger the imagination of man, yet every year the land pours into the sea more that 286,000 cubic miles of water. For century upon century and millennium after millennium, this has been going on, and the sea has not increased its level by so much as one inch. How is this?

We call it the cycle of evaporation and precipitation. The writer of Ecclesiastes said that the ocean maintains its level in spite of this stupendous annual influx, because *the rivers go back to the place from whence they came.* Indeed, they do. As the hurrying, singing, cheerful beads of water go slipping down the toboggan slide of the mountain slope, they hasten impatiently to the sea. There they climb upon the Creator's elevator of evaporation, to form themselves into fleecy clouds of H_2O dust and ride back to the head of their toboggan slide, there to begin their happy, tumbling journey over again.

In the modern science of meteorology all of this is understood and its laws are comprehended. Modern science has fathomed the mystery of this cycle. How did the writer of Ecclesiastes find it out? Again, the casual reader says, "Coincidence."

This reminds us that some years ago there was an Irishman who did not believe in miracles. The parish priest was much concerned with the infidelity of his parishioner, and sought to reason with him as to the reality of the miraculous. The priest opened the conversation by saying, "Now, Pat, you don't believe in miracles; but supposing that on Monday morning as you were carrying the hod to the tenth story of a great building, at just ten o'clock you slipped and fell and landed on your head on the sidewalk so far below. If you arose utterly unhurt, wouldn't that be a miracle?"

"No," said Pat, with a shake of his head, "that would be an accident."

The priest smiled and said, "All right, that is an accident. But supposing the second morning at the same hour of ten o'clock you fell from the same place and again struck the sidewalk, to arise uninjured, wouldn't that be a miracle?"

The Irishman pondered a moment and then said, "No, sir, that would be a coincidence."

Pressing the attack, the priest said, "All right, now we have an accident and a coincidence. But suppose it happened again a third morning. Wouldn't that be a miracle?"

With a twinkle in his eye, the Irishman said, "By that time it would be a habit."

We would be willing to concede six or eight or a dozen of these coincidences, but when they begin to multiply and number scores, some other explanation must be found. And we have not spoken with any semblance of exaggeration when we said scores, for there are in the word of God literally scores of these anticipations of our so-called modern science.

There have been various attempts by interested students of the Scripture to show here and there in the ancient prophecies an indication of the fact that men would some day take to themselves wings like a bird and cleave their way through the air. We would not add to the far-fetched and strained interpretations of Scripture, but there seems to be one place at least where the modern phenomenon of flight was anticipated by the prophetic Scripture.

In the sixtieth chapter of Isaiah, in verse eight, we read, "Who are these that fly as a cloud and as the doves to their windows?" This common rendition of the King James version is perhaps not as clear as some of the more literal translations of the Scripture. It may be just a trifle more specific if this ambiguous passage were translated: "Who are these that fly in air through a cloud and settle as doves to their windows?" It is utterly impossible for any modern man to say who was the first of our race to dream of the possibility and prospect of flying. There are legends and traditions going far back into a mossy antiquity that carry this long frustrated hope of the human heart. It may even be that as Adam basked on a grassy slope in Eden's garden, watching the birds glide from tree to tree and soar high into the cerulean vault, he also said in his heart, "I wish that I could do that."

At any rate, Isaiah has anticipated by the spirit of prophecy the fulfillment of that great hope. If Isaiah were alive today and were to express this question, namely, "Who are these that fly through the clouds?" we would brightly answer, "These are they of the twentieth century." That much of the anticipation at least is established, and we are well on the way toward the climax of his prophecy. The same writer who said that a company of men would fly through the clouds also said they would land like doves at their windows. One of the great drawbacks of aviation today is the high landing speed of airplanes. Because of the necessity for a vast area to form an airport, much of the time that is saved by air travel is lost getting from the cities to the airports and back again. The same ingenious generation who fly will learn also to land at the private openings of their own domiciles.

We merely call attention to the fact that among the weighty and mighty words of this man who was the voice of God in his generation, anticipating the redemption of Calvary and the coming of Him by Whose stripes we are healed, he nevertheless interjected into his prophecy a preview of an age when the air would be vibrant with man-made wings carrying a generation of human beings on their flight through the atmosphere.

The modern science of medicine sets a high value upon prophylaxis, and to us of this generation, prevention means more than cure. It would be mere folly even to suggest that Moses, in the fifteenth century before Christ, knew anything of the germ theory of disease. In our generation, however, this so-called germ theory is no longer a theory; it is an established fact.

Teeming in the atmosphere, found on dust, in water, permeating all foods, and contaminating every physical substance on the planet earth, there are uncountable myriads of pathogenic organisms that cause suffering and sickness in the human body. These tiny creatures that are classified as germs, bacteria, or bacilli, are so infinitely microscopic that the human eye cannot possibly apprehend them unless they are magnified by the lens of a high-powered microscope. In fact, most of them are visible only through an oil immersion lens, which increases their magnitude by many diameters. It is utterly impossible that any human being could have known of the presence of these disease-causing organisms until the great Louis Pasteur established their reality in the face of the opposition of almost every man of science of his generation. These organisms are visible only through the microscope, and until this aid to man's research was invented and well nigh perfected, the bacteria remained unknown.

But now that we know of their existence and have the science of bacteriology that studies their very nature, substance, structure, and organization, physicians almost make a fetish of prophylaxis. Undoubtedly the reader has seen surgeons preparing to enter the operating theatre. The first stage in their preparation, after they have gowned themselves in the white robe and covered their hair with a surgical cap, is to spend twenty minutes washing their hands, from the finger tips to the elbows, with our old familiar friend, green soap. With a scrubbing brush, hot water, and this slimy substance, the surgeon scrubs and works and rinses and scrubs again, until his hands are as nearly sterile as they can be. These clean hands are then wrapped in a sterile towel, that they might not be contaminated by the air, and the nurse binds over the doctor's mouth and nose a sterile gauze pad.

The patient having been made ready for the incision, the sterilized instruments are taken out of the sterilizing machine, and the doctor bends to make his incision of mercy. Perhaps the most important step in all this prophylaxis is the gauze pad that the nurse has bound over his mouth and nose. Many of these pathogenic organisms ride invisibly on the human breath, and the doctor who is operating upon some patient whose life he hopes to save, might breathe infection into the open wound, without the aid of that pad. These tiny organisms, however, cannot pass through the numbers of layers of dry and filmy gauze that constitute the pad, but are trapped and rendered innocuous.

There was an element of intelligence, at least, in the sanitation law that caused all of us to walk around during the dread epidemic of influenza wearing what was commonly called a "flu mask." Some day an intelligent generation will force all who have that weird contagion called the common cold, to wear such a public protective measure when they venture out among their fellow men. This custom, of course, of protecting the innocent from infection by the use of the white cloth, is a highly modern method of preventive medicine. It is based upon the certainty that pathogenic organisms do cause disease in the human body.

How, then, can we account, on purely human grounds, for the use of this same method for the prevention of infection in the days of Moses? In the thirteenth chapter of Leviticus, the forty-fifth verse, we have a record of a contagious disease particularly repulsive to the people of that time. Among other methods for the prevention of the spread of this infection, the law of God, as given through Moses, contained the injunction that the infected man must bind a cloth across his upper lip, *exactly as the physician in the hospital wears the mask today!*

Could Moses have known the germ theory of disease? Not unless he had a microscope that was remarkably modern in its equipment and powers, in which case Moses, and not Pasteur, should be the titular deity of modern medicine. If, however, Moses really spoke by the inspiration of the Spirit of God and transmitted to us only those things which he in turn had received, we have a sensible explanation for this marvelous anticipation of modern wisdom in this ancient book.

One of the oldest criticisms that has ever been directed against the scientific integrity of the Bible, is the objection of a generation ago which criticized the scientific accuracy of the first chapter of Genesis. In this chapter it is specifically stated that life occurred on the planet before the work of God on the fourth day had caused the direct rays of the sun to shine upon the face of this globe. The opponent of the Scripture customarily begins his objection by stating that Moses said there was life before there was light, and this would be an impossibility in science.

We would hasten to refer the reader to the first chapter of Genesis, however, that he might read for himself the exact statement of the factors in the problem. Light illumined the planet on the *first day* of creation. The second day was given up to the establishment of the laws of meteorology that guide and direct what we call weather. On the third day three mighty works were wrought. The oceans were gathered together into their one bed, the vast realm of botany was born, and the world of biology came into being. Up to this time, the light that had been shining on the planet had been filtered through that aqueous envelope which had not yet been dissipated. Then on the fourth day, the atmosphere cleared so that the direct rays of the sun reached the planet with all the brightness characteristic of our modern daylight.

The argument based upon a misconception of this paragraph and a misunderstanding of science, however, is that it would be impossible to have life before the fourth day of creation. We would hasten to reply that the conclusion is too broad to be established in science. *In fact, there is life that cannot exist where there is light!* This may clearly be shown by the recital of an instance that occurred a number of years ago, when the United States Geodetic Survey was first exploring the Carlsbad Caverns and preparing them for the enjoyment of the general public. Dr. Willis T. Lee, who was in charge of the work, made a statement to the effect that "in the dark and gloomy recesses of these incredible caverns no life of any kind" existed.

Immediately a number of eminent biologists leaped upon this utterance and stated that they would never agree to so broad a generalization until it had been scientifically established. They said that no matter how dark and gloomy the depths of those caves might be, with water and atmosphere present it would be impossible to have biological sterility. The author was fortunate enough to be one of the small company who penetrated those black recesses long before they were opened to the public. In a very simple biological survey, of course, we know that near the mouth of the caverns vast numbers of flying mammals called bats have their habitation, and they in turn perhaps are also inhabited by various forms of life! They, however, live where the influence of light is felt.

In the examination of the recesses of the caverns, our party worked most of the time in utter darkness. Specimens of water were taken in three kinds of containers. One was made of a clear flint glass, the second was made of an amber material which had a value of about the density of a Wratten K 3 filter, and the third receptacle consisted of little lead flasks with a screw top. We found in the waters in the black, gloomy recesses of the caves several common types of protozoa.

These creatures not only lived where there was no light, but when they were brought out into the brightness of the day they withered and perished from the effects of the sunlight. The only specimens that we finally got alive to the laboratory were those which were contained in the lead flasks, which, of course, were impervious to light.

Both of the foundations of the argument collapse. There was light before the fourth day of Genesis. Also, there is life that can live without light; in fact, there is life that perishes under the direct influence of light. We would hasten to say that we are not thus arguing for the biological wisdom of the man Moses. We do not dream for an instant that Moses knew anything about protozoology, and perhaps his knowledge even of botany was limited to that of his own generation. The point that we seek to make, however, is that when the Spirit of God inspired Moses to write the records of Genesis, Moses was not restricted to his own wisdom. By the illumination of the Holy Ghost, he wrote things as they are and not as man thought them to be. This same basic premise could be called the thesis of this entire chapter. Certainly it could be applied to every writer of the Old Testament or the New.

Many years ago, the writer sat in a classroom and engaged in a friendly debate with one of his professors in that school. Holding that the Bible was the Word of God, the writer, then a student, was frequently challenged by this instructor, who was a confirmed infidel. We could count on a friendly sparring match almost any time this particular class convened. The professor insistently sought for fallacies and mistakes in the Scripture, which he gleefully advanced in the course of classroom discussion.

On this occasion we remember coming into the classroom and being warned by the twinkle of delight in the good doctor's eye. We felt sure that he had one that day that was unusually satisfactory to himself.

Scarcely had the class convened, when the professor opened up by saying, "Do you still believe the Bible is the Word of God?"

We laughed and said, "Yes, I believe the Bible to be the Word of God, but I am not being still about it."

With his usual reply, the doctor said, "How can you accept the Bible as the Word of God, when it contains such glaring scientific errors?"

We reminded the professor that he had not been able to establish any of those errors so far, and asked what he had now.

He replied by saying, "How about that cytological error that Paul the Apostle made in the fifteenth chapter of First Corinthians?"

Confessing ignorance of the error, we asked the professor to cite it, and he read these words, "All flesh is not the same flesh: but there is one kind of flesh of men, another flesh of beasts, another of fishes, and another of birds."

Very specifically that passage does say that there is a different kind of flesh for men than there is for beasts, and that the flesh of fishes differs from the flesh of birds, and each differs from the other. We were willing to concede the professor's point, that the Bible there stated a biological and cytological difference between the cell structure of the various great phyla.

The professor was somewhat amused when we replied that we agreed with Paul the Apostle that there was a specific and scientific difference between the flesh of one great species and another.

In some surprise the instructor asked, "Have you come this far in your studies, and have you not learned the continuity theory?"

"Oh yes," we said, "we have learned the continuity theory, but we are not giving up the Bible for any theory. It is facts upon which we depend."

The professor warmly insisted that the continuity theory was an established fact.

Since we are speaking now of the archaic days of biology, something more than twenty years ago, it might be wise to remind the reader of this famed continuity theory. This idea was predicated upon the supposition that all cell structure was the same. Early investigators discovered that the cells of all living creatures contained a basic substance called protoplasm. They jumped to the conclusion that all protoplasm was the same, therefore, that all cells were the same. Thus they built up the evolutionary hypothesis that by a continuity of life transmission from one form to another, the various species had arrived through an evolvular process.

We can still remember the warmth of the discussion that followed the criticism of Paul's statement, which repudiated this continuity theory.

The professor said, "The continuity theory is a fact."

We replied, "I don't believe it. I believe that there is a specific and scientific difference between the basic structure of every two groups of living creatures."

He added his usual crushing retort, "Prove it."

We honestly said, "That's the trouble; I can't prove it. But, Professor, after all, I don't have to prove it, because you agree with Paul and me, and admit that we are right."

In stuttering chagrin, the professor said, "But I don't agree; I am standing here denying it."

Trusting that his sense of humor would stand the strain, we took a chance and retorted, "Yes, that's what you say now, but actions speak louder than words. You *do* agree with us that all flesh is not the same flesh. For instance, let us assume that you ate your dinner today in the Palace Hotel and ordered quail on toast, for which you were charged. If they served you codfish, you would yell loudly enough to be heard across the Bay of San Francisco."

Somewhat bewildered, the good doctor said, "What does that prove?"

Not having any credits left in that class and thus being able to take tremendous chances, we replied, "That proves that while *you* might not know the difference between a fish and a bird, your stomach and your taste buds do, and it seems, then, as though we have more sense under our belts than we have under our hats."

The argument broke up in an uproar, and neither of us ever convinced the other. How we wish that the doctor were alive today! We would like to go to him in a sweet kindly spirit and pointing at him an index finger we would like to say, "Aha!" with all the emphasis that could be put upon that ejaculation. For now according to the findings of modern science Paul the Apostle should be classified as a very credible cytologist! You may perhaps have read of that interesting reagent produced by the Parke Davis laboratories and named, upon its introduction, "Anti-human Precipitin." This has been largely used by the scientific sections of criminal investigation departments in all of our big city police systems.

If one had a bit of bone, or blood, or flesh, or skin, or organic substance that was alive or had been alive, no matter how old or dessicated that substance might be, and one desired to know from what living creature it had come, the method would be comparatively simple. There was a time when murderers, faced with the evidence of a blood-stained garment, had some ability to evade justice by maintaining that they had killed a rabbit or a chicken or some other meat animal, and the law could not prove the contrary. Those days are gone forever. If we had dried blood, the stain of blood, or live blood, and we put it into the test tube and added the anti-human precipitin, we would get an almost instant reaction which said

"This is animal" or "This is human."

The same is true of all the cell structure of the human body. This reagent will not tell the difference between two kinds of animals. It will not tell the difference between two varieties of man, but it will instantly and infallibly indicate whether the once living matter which is under investigation came from an animal or from a human being. If the indication shows that it is human, there the investigation stops, for there is no scientific technique by which we may determine the difference between two varieties of the human species. If, however, the indication is that it is animal, there are cytological means of differentiation by which the kind of animal may be classified.

In other words, if we were asked to express the latest findings of the cytology of our generation, we could do no better than to turn to First Corinthians the fifteenth chapter, and read verse thirty-nine, "All flesh is not the same flesh." There *is* one kind of flesh for man and a different kind of flesh for the animals, the birds, and all other living creatures.

Again we ask how Paul the Apostle could have known this. The answer is simple: he did not know and could not have known. The only possible explanation for his anticipation of this modern wisdom, then, is to concede that he spoke and wrote as he was moved by the Spirit of God. Thus the Almighty in revealing His will for our generation anticipated the wisdom of our day, that His Book might be in absolute harmony with the advancing wisdom of men.

The foregoing illustration very naturally and logically suggests the equally remarkable fashion in which this same writer, Paul the Apostle, has uttered conclusions in harmony with our modern science of anthropology. In his magnificent address to the Areopagites, preserved for us in the seventeenth chapter of Acts, this great logician offers seven reasons for saying that man can find God and truly apprehend Him. The third reason in this series of seven is the argument from anthropology. The Authorized Version presents the argument in these words, "And hath made of one blood all nations of men that dwell on all the face of the earth."

It is a fact that the word "blood" is not found in many of the old manuscripts of the New Testament. For this reason it is omitted from the American Revised Version, which merely states, "And hath made of one every nation of men to dwell on all the face of the earth." Using the more familiar version that is known as the Authorized, we can find no present scientific argument with this statement of Paul the Apostle. If an inquirer should bring into the laboratory adapted for this type of work, seven drops of blood, and should ask for the classification of each specimen of blood, the problem would be simple for the worker who is trained in this field of science.

If these seven drops of blood had come from the veins of a horse, a cow, a sheep, a goat, a chicken, an ape, and a man, a scientific investigation requiring only a relatively few minutes would show positively from which kind of creature each specimen of blood had come.

If, however, the same investigator should bring into the laboratory seven drops of human blood and should ask for a classification of mankind from these drops of blood, he would seek such information in vain. It is utterly impossible to tell the difference, by any now known technique, between the blood of a Chinese and an Anglo-Saxon. It is equally impossible to tell the difference between the blood of a German and a Japanese. Scotch, Irish, English, African, Mongoloid, or Caucasian — they are all just human blood. There is no known method of analysis that will teach us anything about the creatures from whom these blood drops were derived, except only the simple conclusion, that he was, in each case, a human being.

If the older rendition should prove to be incorrect, and the right statement is, "God hath made of one every race of men," anthropology can still find no fault with whatever that "one" is intended to be. Anthropology recognizes one genus, namely, the genus homo. Of the genus homo, there is only one known species, the species sapiens. Therefore, man is classified as the homo sapiens, regardless of the color of his skin, his so-called racial distribution, or peculiarity of vocabulary. One species, of which there are several recognized varieties, is the latest dictum of the science of anthropology.

Did Paul know this? In the day when he walked the earth, race prejudice had perhaps reached its highest development, because of the pride resident in Roman psychology. Yet this man who was born a Roman, anticipating all of the wisdom of our generation as far as it might be applied to the species that is called man, arrived by inspiration at the same conclusion that we have established by research.

There is no field of investigation open to men that has been so thoroughly explored in the past few years as has the field of blood. A long time ago, going back through the hundreds of years and into the thousands, our present conclusions concerning the essential nature of the blood were anticipated in the seventeenth chapter of Leviticus. If the reader would take time to refer to this chapter, he would find that the Children of Israel were forbidden to eat any manner of blood. The penalty for the violation of this prohibition was that the soul of the man who ate blood should be cut off from among the people.

This commandment is repeated and reiterated on the specific ground that the life of the flesh is the blood thereof. Three times this scientific dictum is repeated in the short space of five verses. Predicated upon this fact there is the further statement that because the life of the flesh is in the blood, the blood has been given upon the altar to make an atonement for our souls, "for it is the blood that maketh an atonement for the soul." In the days when Moses lived and wrote, very little was known about the laws of blood circulation, the composition of blood, and the marvelous system of blood distribution. Indeed, we can read in medical journals only a few generations old and meet with surprising ignorance concerning the nature and purpose and function of blood.

In those days when it was the universal practice to bleed the patient (before he got his bill), one author has ingeniously suggested that in the letting of blood the practitioner should carefully weigh and measure the amount of blood taken from one arm. He was then enjoined to remove carefully the same amount from the opposite arm, on the ground that if more blood were let from one side of the body than from the other, the body would thus become lopsided and the blood supply unbalanced! In the days when Moses walked the earth, according to the ancient legends, men believed that arteries were air passages which permeated the body. It would be fantastic to suppose that Moses or any of his contemporaries were in possession of our knowledge concerning the nature, analysis, and function of the blood. Yet any one who has ever suffered from pernicious anemia would indeed concede the truth of the statement that the life is in the blood. When the blood dies, the individual dies. Long before the immortal Harvey had done his pioneering work that made possible our present body of knowledge in this sphere of medical practice. Moses had anticipated the conclusions of our present day!

The life of the flesh, indeed, *is* in the blood!

If this be so, and the premise is thus established, then the conclusion that is based upon that premise is equally authoritative.

The conclusion is that since the life of the flesh is in the blood, atonement is in the blood as well.

That one who finds in Calvary his source of salvation is not only Scripturally justified, but is thus scientifically vindicated as well.

The life of the flesh is in the blood which permeates the flesh.

The life of the soul is in the blood that was shed when the flesh of the Son of God was riven and broken on Calvary's cross for the sins of men.

Returning from this digression, we would point again to the astonishing fact that a modern premise of accepted therapy, which was achieved as a goal of extended research, was anticipated by the writer of Leviticus more than three thousand years before modernity made this discovery.

Can there be any other explanation of this strange phenomenon than the one that is offered by Peter, namely, "Holy men of old spake as they were moved by the Spirit of God"? Indeed, we know not any!

Modern Science in an Ancient Book

CHAPTER IV

Modern Science in an Ancient Book

WE have introduced in our previous chapter a sufficient number of illustrations to obviate the possibility of coincidence in the anticipation of the scientific discoveries of our generation by the writers of the Bible. We would now proceed to make the case more conclusive by citing an amazing number of such instances from one single chapter of the Scripture, in the book that bears the name of Job. It is possible that unless new evidence from archeological sources should be discovered, we will never be able to establish the moot question of the exact date of the writing of the book of Job. Certainly nobody who is within ten years of being up to date in the matter of evidence, would any longer accept the exploded myths of the higher critical school which customarily assigned the book of Job to an unknown scribe who lived in the days of Hezekiah. The book of Job was unquestionably written very close to the period of Abraham, and is one of the oldest manuscripts in the collection of inspired literature that is called the Bible.

Job was a real person, who suffered real disasters and who had a real experience in God's dealings with men. In the course of his earlier pronouncements, Job made a statement concerning God that expressed unlimited confidence in His wisdom and power. In the second verse of the ninth chapter, the patriarch said, "How can a man justify himself before God? If he will contend with Him, he cannot answer Him one of a thousand." This is perhaps the most marvelous tribute to the unlimited knowledge of the great Teacher that is found in the entire Book. The pupil who cannot answer one question in a thousand would, of course, confess his tremendous inferiority to the teacher.

Later, irritated by the contentions of his dubious friends, Job, apparently turning from his former position, made a complaint before God and an appeal to Him. In the twenty-third chapter he said, "O that I knew where I might find Him, that I might come even to His feet. I would order my cause before Him and fill my mouth with arguments. I would know the words wherewith He would answer me and I would understand what He would say unto me." To put it in the bold, blunt, plain diction of modern speech, Job, disgusted with men, said that he would like to have a chance to argue this matter with God. Apparently he had for a moment forgotten his previous assertion that if God should give an examination to man, man could not answer Him one question in a thousand.

Some years ago the writer was attending a group meeting of a scientific convention. Seated around the table were a dozen or fifteen men, representing various interests in this particular field of research. When the luncheon was over and the program had been discussed, with that good-humored banter that marks this type of gathering, several of the other men were having some hilarious fun because of the antiquated and childish ideas of inspiration maintained by the writer. Since the fun was good-natured and since we have always believed that a calf with plenty of rope will hang itself, we rejoined in the same mild sarcastic fashion and entered into the enjoyment of the occasion.

Surely enough, the argument had not gone along very far before one of the men suggested that it would be amusing and interesting if we could compare our learning in this generation with the current knowledge of those Biblical writers. Seizing the opportunity, this writer said, "Perhaps you gentlemen remember an ancient patriarch by the name of Job? In one of his outbursts, he said to his friends, 'No doubt ye are the people, and wisdom will perish with you.' How unfortunate that Job could not have known you gentlemen. He could have said this same thing without any element of sarcasm."

One of the company rather crisply replied, "At least, we know a lot more than Job did!"

Seeing that the trap was eagerly invaded, we sprung it with this retort, "I sometimes wonder. Do you gentlemen know that at one time Job himself said, 'I would like to argue my case before God; I would like to stand an examination.' Apparently the Lord was listening, for

He gave Job an examination consisting of forty scientific questions. Job could not answer one! I wonder how much more we know about those things than the prophet Job did."

At once there was an eager surge of response, a number of men saying they would like to take that examination. Time being heavy on our hands, we sent a bell-boy upstairs for a Gideon Bible, and when he returned we proposed to take that examination. Enjoying the humor of the situation, the writer suggested, "I will read the questions and you fellows write out your answers. I am inclined to think you would not even know where to find the questions! Let us agree, for the sake of convenience, that since there are forty questions, we allow ten points to each question. If a man gets a question right, he gets ten points on that question, making four hundred for a perfect examination. Since each question is in two divisions, let's decide that if half the question is answered correctly five points will be allowed for that much success."

The conditions were agreed upon and the examination taken.

The smartest man around that table made thirty-five out of a possible four hundred!

It might be interesting to conclude that we owe a great deal to the marvelous advance of learning in the last four thousand years, on the ground that this learning has taught us three and one-half things that Job did not know! That conclusion, of course, not only would be unkind but it would also be incorrect. We have learned much that Job did not know. The fact still remains, however, that in the thirty-eighth chapter of Job there are forty magnificent anticipations of the physical science with which we deal today that were utterly beyond the power of Job even to phrase or express. When Job said, "I would like to argue my case with God," the Lord evidently was listening, for the thirty-eighth chapter of Job begins with the words, "Then the Lord answered Job out of the whirlwind, and said, "Who is this that darkeneth counsel by words without knowledge? Gird up now thy loins like a man; for I will demand of thee, and answer thou me." There is an element of humor in the very introduction. Job said he would like to argue with God. God answered: "I will now give you an oral examination." To this Job replied, "I am ready; start the questions."

In the very first question the Almighty Creator of the heaven and the earth laid Job flat and prostrate with the simple words, "Where wast thou when I laid the foundations of the earth?"

The centuries have rolled away since that question was asked of Job, and indeed they have multiplied themselves into millenniums that have been born and died. Yet no man today can answer that question which God asked Job any better than the prophet himself answered in his day. The science of embryology is indeed a recent advance in man's learning. It is not too much to say that there was no real embryology before the twentieth century. The author has among his prized possessions of antiquity a treatise on embryology written by Salmon in the year 1790. It is a most fascinating entertainment to compare that ancient text with the known and established facts of the science of embryology in our generation.

Yet with all of our advancing wisdom, there is no man today who can answer that question that the Lord God asked Job, "Where were you when the foundations of the earth were laid?" The wisdom of India contends for eternal life without beginning and without ending. According to their teachings, this life is reincarnated through successive aeons of time in many births and deaths.

Other schools of thought, while not calling themselves re-incarnationists, hold that since soul life or spirit life is indestructible, there are perhaps a certain limited number of spirits that go through cycles of living, appearing on the planet again and again. Many men of science hold that matter, including life, is indestructible.

Be that as it may, we are still at a loss to say at what point and where and when our personalities entered into the stream of eternal existence. We understand through Christian theology that when a man accepts Jesus Christ as His Saviour and is regenerated, he then becomes an integral part of the stream of everlasting life. That stream has no beginning and no ending.

When a mountain rill flows into the Mississippi River, the waters of that stream are so incorporated with the substance of the river that no man can separate one from the other. The mountain stream still lives in the vaster life of the majestic river. After the mountain rill has entered the major stream, no man can later pick out a specimen of water and say from which of the many feeders that particular specimen came. As the Father of Waters rolls grandly by the site of New Orleans, it is simply the mighty Mississippi composed of innumerable, uncountable individual drops. It is one cohesive stream. Regardless of its infinite sources, it has been amalgamated into one uniform body. So when the individual by regeneration is united to the life of God, he becomes part of eternity, and cannot say when his life began nor when it will end. Metaphysically speaking, then, to our everlasting life there is neither beginning nor ending.

Again, in the science of embryology, there is no living authority who can say whence the quickening life comes that brings conscious existence into the cell mass that is called the fetus. The major mystery in this complicated science is the coming of that life which is called soul, or spirit, and which animates the mass of biological substance with intelligent entity, comprehension, and the functions of will.

No man can understand this mystery, nor can any man say with certainty, "I was not in existence when the foundations of the earth were laid." We cannot say whence this life was derived, hence we do not know from what point its existence is dated. Perhaps the greatest mystery of the laboratory today is the enigma of life. We can only say we have it and lose it. The life we lay down here goes on somewhere, somehow. We may have had it before. No man can prove this contention either way.

So with the superior knowledge of this twentieth century after Christ, we look back into the twentieth century before Him, and hear Job say in humility before God, "I do not know." Crestfallen, we can only join in the chorus and say, "Move over, Job, I want to occupy that bed with you."

The other half of that question is equally impossible for man to answer, as we have showed in the previous chapter. What are these foundations of the earth that are here mentioned? We know the size of the globe on which we dwell, and have been able to compute its specific weight. If we had had a hook whereupon to hang a ball of the size and weight of this earth, it would take, in round numbers, three hundred million miles of one-inch steel cable to bear the weight of this suspended globe. That is, of course, provided we had something or some place whereupon to hang it!

There was a sheepish smile upon the faces of the men who took the examination, as they pondered this question and then suggested that we pass on to the next one. The second question that we dwelt upon that day, and that we now lay before the mind of the reader, is found in the seventh verse of this chapter: "When the morning stars sang together, and all the sons of God shouted for joy?" How did Job know that at the dawn of creation the morning stars sang together, and all the sons of God shouted for joy? At one time it was futilely attempted to evade this question by suggesting that this was poetic imagination on the part of Job. "Of course, stars do not sing!" we said. That notion, however, will no longer obtain in the generation in which we live, for through the marvels of modern physics we have learned many things about the tonal value of light.

Light and color and sound are fundamentally the same. There are rays of waves of some tangible substance pulsating across or through space. Some of these beats reach the eye as light, some reach the eye as color, and some reach the ear as sound. The mathematics and the physics of light and sound are now so closely interrelated that in the laboratories of research you may see almost fabulous demonstrations of the unity of nature of light, color and sound.

There are rays of color so slow and so long that the eye cannot see them. All of these long rays are grouped from the infra-red down. There are other rays of colors so fast and so short that the eye cannot apprehend them. These we group from the ultra-violet up. We have photographic plates and optical apparatus which will capture these rays and make them serve the human eye. Now exactly as there are color rays that cannot reach the eye, so there are also sound waves which do not reach the ear. Recent experiments have convinced the physicist that every ray of light as well as every shade of color has a definite phonetic value. The light of the sun or the light of the stars speeding through space carries with it a note of sound. If our ears were tuned to hear these melodies, we too could enjoy the music of the spheres. Job was scientifically and academically correct when he said that the morning stars sang together in the instance of creation, for where light is, sound accompanies it.

Perhaps the reader has seen the famous color organ now operating in the dining quarters of the new Radio Center in New York City. There upon the dome above the diners and the dancers, soft and marvelous colors blend and cross each other in ceaseless play, as the notes of an organ caress the ear. These brilliant rainbows are occasioned by transmitting the sounds of the organ into the equivalent color value of each note of the scale. This value is constant. The phonetic value and the color value of a given note never vary. So as the light rays blend their colors in a fantasy of brilliant splendor, the melody of these same physical rays enchants the ear in an equally delightful harmony of sound.

We are all familiar with the phenomenon of "talking film". Upon the inanimate strip of film there are forms or divisions of pictures.

By the side of these frames there is a jagged, serrated line which is commonly called the sound track. When this film is set in motion before a light source in a projector, one beam of light passes through the picture and the sound track. This beam of light casts upon the screen the animated action of the scene. This same beam of light, by the aid of the modern Aladdin's lamp called the photo-electric cell, is transmuted into sound. So the one light source brings to the delighted eye of the beholder all the movement and action of the film, while at the same time it brings to his ear the conversation, the melody of song, and the accompaniment of a philharmonic orchestra!

It would be the crassest folly to suggest that Job knew this. Of course he did not. But when the stars were created and their light rays of varying lengths swept out across the void of sidereal space, they blended into a harmony which *might* be apprehended by ears attuned to shorter wave lengths than the ears of humanity. Of this we cannot be sure. Our only certainty now comes from the science of physics. Either Job anticipated all of this marvelous knowledge, or else the Spirit of God directed to Job these queries that are beyond our power to comprehend.

If we may paraphrase the next question for the sake of simplicity, we would put it in these words, "What is the mysterious force that holds the sea within its bounds?" The entire wording of the query is one of the most magnificent prose poems in literature. We give it here in the words of Job thirty-eight: "Or who shut up the sea with doors, when it brake forth, as if it had issued out of the womb? When I made the cloud the garment thereof, and thick darkness a swaddlingband for it." In the course of the question, Job draws a picture of the magnitude and the might of God that is never exceeded in the pages of the Bible. The Almighty is here depicted as a midwife who officiated at the birth of the sea. In the graphic imagery of this paragraph, God is pictured as sitting down and taking upon His lap the new-born ocean. With one hand He grasped thick darkness to make a flannel band for the new baby's tummy, and with the other He seized the clouds and wove them into a flannel nightie to cover its little form! Carefully he concludes its imagery by saying that God then broke up for it His decreed place and set doors and bars, and said, "Hitherto shalt thou come, but no further; and here shall thy proud waves be stayed."

We hasten to state that we are very glad for the obedience of the ocean. When God put it in the cradle of the deep and said, "Now stay there," the obedient but mighty infant remained in that bed to this present day. Unlike our children, who quickly seek to leave the cradle and romp about the floor, the ocean has stayed put. Once in a while it seems a bit restless as it murmurs against these bars.

It was only a short while ago that the author was engaged in some summer lecture work on Long Island. The sea went on a rampage and hammered with mighty force against the shores of that region. Houses caved in, breakwaters were shattered, highways were torn asunder, and devastation strewed the beach mile after mile. The papers said that it was one of the worst storms in generations. That was rather humorous. We contented ourselves with the cryptic observation that the baby just slobbered a bit! But if he ever felt his strength and left his cradle to take a walk across the surrounding terrain, he would hammer the works of man flat to the earth in a few passing minutes.

Seriously now, what is it that holds the sea in place? This question no man can answer. We may speak learnedly about the effect that the sun, moon, and stars have upon the tides of the sea. We may use great swelling words to speak of the effect of the law of gravity, and shroud our ignorance in verbosity, but the simple fact of the matter is that the force which controls the sea is still beyond the understanding of men, though we have often tried to solve its mystery. In times gone by there have been occasions when the sea burst forth from its bounds, overstepped its bonds, and devastated regions. There are traditions of continents submerged, empires and dynasties wiped out. While the sea is calm and remains within its boundaries, it is the friend of man.

Who holds its powerful forces in subjection? Men have often pondered this mystery, and some weird answers have come to us from antiquity. We are familiar with the ancient Persian teaching that the earth was flat and shaped like a warrior's shield. All around the edge of the shield, they postulated the range of mountains which their cartographers called the "Mountains of Caif." The purpose of this rectangular range of mountains was to hold the sea in place on this flat earth, lest it flow off the edge and the ocean become dry!

Many other weird theories were advanced by men of past generations. Job, however, makes no such wild guess. Recognizing the sovereignty of God, he is content with the statement of deity, "*I* set bars and doors, and said, 'Thus far and no farther'." Does modern science have a better explanation? If so, we have never heard it.

As a quaint sidelight upon this odd but intriguing series of questions, we would cite the twelfth verse, "Hast thou commanded the morning since thy days began?" How many times have we longed to take up this quotation; how many times have we longed to be able to reply in the affirmative! Have you ever been afraid in the dark? What would you then have given to have been able to command the daylight? Have you ever suffered pain at night? Have you ever waited for the dawn while it crawled on its inexorable path with leaden feet? Did you then command the day?

Some time ago we were with an expedition in the vast, far-flung wilderness of a mountain region. About nine o'clock one night the pangs of toothache suddenly assailed us. It was one of those "shut in" toothaches that center in an apparently sound tooth. No relief was possible. Until two o'clock in the morning we tried in vain to quiet this extreme inconvenience, and then we saddled our horse and rode to a village across the mountains in the valley beyond. It was two hours before the earliest break of dawn when we arrived in the mountain hamlet. There was no possibility of finding a dentist until one hour after sunrise at the very earliest. "Hast thou commanded the morning since thy days began?" We would have given all the money that we had on our person at that time, if we could have said to the reluctant daylight, "Speed up, dawn, and come right now!"

The hour of dawn changes from day to day. The very second of daybreak changes each succeeding day. How is this kept in order; and who regulates this clock of God? Who cleans its wheels and makes those minor repairs which bring the daylight on its predetermined schedule, with more than human punctuality? There is a tremendous suggestion in this question. Battles have been lost for lack of light. Empires have fallen and dynasties have arisen because no man could advance or delay the coming of dawn. Who makes the day to know its place and hour? Can a man learn this secret?

In our pockets we carry time-pieces that divide our day and night into minutes and seconds. That is to say, the wheels and springs of our chronometers have been devised by thinking men to keep pace with astronomical bodies. So vast in size and in such gigantic magnitude are they, that this earth of ours compares to them at about the same ratio that one drop of water would compare to the Pacific Ocean. Yet the wheels of our time pieces must travel with them at their same pace, subject to minor corrections.

We would call the reader's attention to the indisputable fact that this earth fits in with a mathematical relationship to every point of light in the entire sidereal system. Who is there among us who has power to command the dawn and to cause the dayspring to know his place? How crass and utterly contemptible is the silly pride of a puny creature like man who dares inveigh against the Almighty, Whose spoken word, "Let there be lights in the firmament of the heaven," is instantly obeyed by the appearance of gigantiae beyond the power of man to comprehend, much less control! Something of the humility of Job should be in the heart of the modern sage as he reads this evidence of infinite wisdom in an ancient book.

One of the interesting sidelights of the ancient culture prevailing in the day of Job, as well as a marvelous anticipation of the wisdom of our day, is found in the fourteenth verse of this examination. Continuing this observation about the dawning of the day, the statement is made that "earth is turned as clay to the seal," this being a continuation of the preceding, or thirteenth, verse of the chapter. In the far-away days of that twentieth century before Christ, it was not customary for men to carry fountain pens and lead pencils wherewith to sign their names and transcribe their thoughts. No reader who has ever visited a museum of archaeology has failed to note the "seals" that were commonly in use in those days. These were generally round, composed of a semi-precious stone or some hard substance in which the signature was engraved in the matrix. This seal, perforated longitudinally and rotating upon a tiny axle of some hard material, was pressed against the face of the damp clay and rotated. As the seal was turned in the face of the clay, it left its inscription. This clay was baked in the furnace and then became a permanent record.

Now see the marvelous illustration of this ingenious question! Out in space, the sun is shining. Its light flows forth without interruption day or night. On an established orbit about that sun, our earth is journeying on her annual orbital revolution. At the same time, the planet is spinning on its axis, turning in the face of the sun like the seal in the face of the clay.

Did Job know this?

The question is too fantastic even for solemn consideration.

Only the Hand which started this orb in motion could have directed the penning of those words forty centuries ago.

One would scarcely expect to find the highly modern science of oceanography introduced into a book four thousand years old, but here it is, in the sixteenth verse: "Hast thou entered into the springs of the sea, or hast thou walked in the recesses of the deep?"

It has been our privilege on several occasions to walk in the recesses of the deep. The first time we walked through the pale green twilight of the sea, it was at a comparatively shallow depth, something less than fifty feet. On that occasion we walked around, observing quaint forms of life on the floor of the Gulf. We can still remember the sudden quickening of our pulse as we stood on the ladder, ready to descend. Over our head was placed a helmet with heavy glass eyes. We waited for the rest of the suit, but we waited in vain! There was a space around our neck and under our chin three inches wide. When the operator controlling the air hose tapped on our helmet with a hammer, giving us the signal to descend, we reached up and signed for him to take off the helmet.

In some glee he asked, "What is the matter, Doctor, did your nerve fail you?"

We replied, "No, but where is the rest of it?"

He said, "This is all you need."

We asked, "What will keep the water from rushing into this empty space when the pressure of the deep pours in?"

He explained that the pressure of the air inside of the helmet would overcome that of the water. Of course, we knew that this would work, theoretically, and even though we were in the helmet, we felt reasonably sure that the operator didn't wish to drown us, so we decided to take the chance! Again the helmet was put over our head and for the first time we descended into the quiet fairyland of the deep. Confidence came with passing time and we found that our mentor was right. No matter what position we assumed, the pressure of the air overcame the thrust of the water, and we could lie down, walk around, and even attempt to stand on our head, in perfect security!

We have never missed an opportunity to repeat the performance since, and there is a space and calm on the floor of the sea that every one should experience. Danger and death are there as well. But even though we may picnic on the ocean floor, no man on the face of the earth has entered into the "springs" of the sea since the days of Job. Many men have walked in the recesses of the deep, but no man has entered into its springs. What and where are these "springs of the deep?" In some parts of the ocean, fresh water may be obtained! There are places where strata and currents of fresh water are known to exist. Some men maintain that these are river streams which have never lost their identity in the sea; other authorities say that they are artesian wells that burst out on the floor of the ocean.

No man knows, and perhaps none ever will know, the ultimate secrets of the ocean floor. A great increase of knowledge has come to us with the work of scientists who deal with the sea, but there are some things that still elude our grasp. One of the greatest institutes for the study of the sea is the Scripps Marine Institute for Biological Survey, located on the California Coast, at the little seaport of La Jolla. We were talking one day with the curator of the museum there, and he told us many fascinating things that ocean biological research had revealed, but there are some things at present that are unfathomable.

He recounted how some years ago a little party of men were studying the types of life to be found at an ocean depth never before attempted. Their apparatus allowed them to go hundreds of fathoms below the surface. They hooked some gigantic leviathan of the deep and started to draw him up with their steel line and steam winch. Slowly they began to bring him in. Hundreds of feet from the surface, their line suddenly went slack, and they said, "We have lost him. Bring in the hook and we will bait up and try again." When the hook came in, they found that they had not lost their catch. Still clinging to the barb was a piece of the mouth and a piece of the head! No man can know or ever will know what the creature was like. He lived at so great a depth, resisting the unthinkable pressure of the ocean floor, that when the pressure was relieved, his muscular energy, constructed to resist tons of pressure, continuing to thrust out against the pressure that no longer existed, literally tore him to pieces!

The life of the deep is not the only mystery that challenges the interest of man. We cannot now know the exact chemical composition of water at that depth. With great hope a company of eminent scientists went one day to find the exact nature of water at the deepest spot then known. Their apparatus was especially constructed to thrust a reinforced brass tube down to a great depth, where a cleverly constructed device was to pull the plug from the tube. This would let the tube fill up with water at that stratum, and the operator would then close the tube with this plug so that no water could leak in from other depths on the way up. Thus they hoped to add the item of chemic contents at vast depths to our knowledge of the ocean.

Alas! The eminent gentlemen came back sadder, but no wiser! For when they thrust their brass tube down to the desired depth, they went through the motions of pulling the plug and closing it again, then gleefully pulled it up. To their chagrin, they learned nothing! For when their "tube" returned, it was a flat sheet of wrinkled brass! The terrible pressure had flattened their tube to the thickness of thin cardboard, and it looked as though it had been hammered and pressed into crinkled metal waves! No man can "enter into the springs of the deep." A little way down we can go, but the ocean floor is the secret place where many mysteries of God remain. It is also probable that they *will remain* mysteries until the day when "the sea gives up its dead." We do not know much more today than Job did about the "springs of the deep." The wonder of this verse lies in the fact that Job, four thousand years ago, even knew that they existed! Or is it just possible that he, too, "spoke as he was moved by the Spirit of God?"

However, we may congratulate ourselves that we *have* learned some things! We can all answer the question in verse eighteen. It is merely a matter of travel and experience. Did you ever notice what a tremendous amount of our boasted "culture" and "modern advancement" are truly mechanical? We are a traveled age. Job was unable to answer when God asked him, "Hast thou comprehended the earth in its breadth?" Job, of course, said, "No." But today many of us have been around the globe, and the rest of us have read enough to be able to answer, "Yes, it is about eight thousand miles in diameter." So we do advance and learn!

We believe one of the most pressing problems that challenged the intellect of primitive man was the problem of how to sit down and go somewhere while resting! Horses were harnessed — oxen were taught to pull great loads — it may be barely possible that the mighty dinosaurs were utilized as the elephant is today; and all that man might travel in comfort and ease! Not satisfied with animal aids, modern man has made himself mechanical beasts of burden. The air is raucous with their brazen toots and metallic growls, and fetid with the stench of exhausted breath from their iron lungs! Taking to ourselves the wings of a dove, we now fly to the isles of the sea. And because we have mastered the problem of speed in travel, we say that we are the most wonderful generation that ever lived.

But with all this new culture, have we really progressed? Are we any closer to God than Job and other patriarchs were? What is the spiritual and eternal value of a mechanical progress? Are we mentally the better for all our modern conveniences? We realize that if Job were suddenly raised in that resurrection to which he looked forward, he would, of course, be confused. But in one hour he could learn to push the white button on the wall when he wanted light, and push the black button when he went to bed. In that same hour he could learn to put in a fuse when the lights went out; and after all, that's about all the average modern knows about electric illumination! It wouldn't take Abraham, the friend of God, more than one hour to learn enough "culture" so that he would not get on a street car until it stopped, and would stay on until it stopped again! And that's more than some folks know now! Every once in a while we see some highly modern, cultured man picking himself up, shaken to pieces, because he tried to get off a car before it stopped!

But we have progressed. Job had never been around the world to survey it; modern man has! With great pride, we take ten points in our examination; we can answer this question, at least!

A notable instance of the anticipation of modern scientific discovery by the ancient writers of the Scripture is found in the twenty-second verse of this chapter. Here God inquires of Job, "Hast thou entered into the treasures of the snow? Or hast thou seen the treasures of the hail?"

This word "treasures" has a very exact significance. Fiction is full of references to buried treasure. Many expeditions have been outfitted to recover the treasure of Captain Kidd, and we always associate financial return with this word "treasure". So the "treasury" of the United States is the place where we keep our national deficit! ! And the "treasurer" is the man who receives funds.

What can possibly be the *treasure* that is connected with snow and with hail? We don't believe Job knew, and certainly no modern writer or reader knew until Dr. Frank T. Shutt, Dominion chemist of the Canadian Department of Agriculture, published the result of his seventeen years of research in the financial worth of snow and hail.

In a recent issue of "Science", a release by "Science Service" recounts the result of Dr. Shutt's experiments. He finds that there is a definite financial value to snow and hail, as they wash out of the atmosphere nitrogenous substances that fertilize the soil. The action of snow and hail centrifuging through the air, deposits upon the land four kinds of chemical fertilizer: free ammonia, nitrates, nitrites, and albuminoid ammonia. These substances, to the value of $14.08 per acre, are deposited in a winter's fall of snow and hail. These are the forms in which the nitrogen of the air can be assimilated by plants, as food. This is the equivalent of forty-four pounds of expensive imported Chilian saltpetre per acre.

If a farmer had ten acres of land under cultivation, the treasure of the snow and the hail for him would be $140.80 per year. If you ascertain the number of acres under cultivation in your state and multiply them by $14.08 per acre, you will learn what the treasure of the snow and the hail really amounts to in your own locality. If you multiply the number of arable acres in North America by this factor, you will get a stupendous sum of real money!

So there is exact significance to this strange suggestion in this chapter of Job. *How did he know?* Either Job, four thousand years ago, knew what the modern scientist has just discovered, or the God Who asked the question really spoke through this Book.

It is manifestly impossible that Job could have known the answer to the question embodied in the twenty-fourth verse; nay, he could not even have framed the question. "By what way is the light parted?" asks the great Questioner; and Job had no reply. The word in the Hebrew, translated into the English as "way", is "derek." It literally means "manner", — or "technique" would be even a better translation. The Hebrew word "chalaq" is translated in the old English "parted", but an equally acceptable sense of "chalaq" is "apportioned."

Let us paraphrase this verse also, and read, "By what technique is the light apportioned?" Now imagine any man asking that question four thousand years ago! It is, of course, a simple one in this day, and the student instantly answers: "By passing it through the prism of the spectroscope." But who could have known that in Job's day? And since it is manifestly impossible for any human mind to frame a question that the mind knows nothing of, a greater than man is the Questioner here!

When we heat a metal red hot, or heat any substance until it is incandescent, it gives forth rays of light. These rays, after passing through the prism of the spectroscope, divide themselves on the graph according to the content of the matter that sent them forth. Thus when a ray of light reaches us from some far-flung star, we need only to pass that light ray through the spectroscope to see the composition of that star, and the proportion of each of its ingredients. This division of light rays is always constant, and does not vary in the least particular, so that we may always rely upon the results. Spectroscopic analysis is an exact science, and this is now the manner by which "the light is apportioned." This places us in a quandary: either Job knew this, or supernatural wisdom is revealed here!

This query concerning the nature and division into mathematical portions of the element that is called light, very logically leads into a series of questions that touch upon the very modern subject of meteorology. In the days of Matthew Fontaine Maury, who was perhaps the greatest man of science who has graced the American Hall of Fame, this science was really born. Other men, both in Europe and at home, collaborated with Maury in the correlation of data, until finally a foundation was laid for the structure that has grown since into a marvelous body of established information. Thus we are almost within touch of the generation that learned the function and purpose of lightning and thunder.

Although the heavens might be dark and overcast with clouds of H_2O dust, freighted with a life-giving fluid for which the thirsty earth was panting in desire, no precipitation would alleviate the dryness of the ground, were it not for the tremendous forces set in operation by the flash and crash of the heavenly artillery. Lightning is essential to the orderly production of precipitation. This fact was advanced as a possible theory, later to become established as an unquestioned principle, almost within reach of our own times. And yet here we have the prophet Job anticipating the wisdom of this age by some four thousand years, for he plainly says that some unknown power, force, or person prepares the way for the lightning and thunder which cause the rain upon the wilderness wherein no man dwells!

There is, of course, an element of humor in that latter suggestion. It might not be too strong a word if we said that it was highly sarcastic on the part of the divine inquisitor. The suggestion is, "You men seem to be able to take care of your cities, after a fashion, but who provides for the wilderness and the beasts that dwell therein?" Certainly the grass must grow in the unpeopled places, or the creatures of the wild cannot eat. Therefore, rain is essential. Certainly water is absolutely essential to the continuity of life in jungle or wilderness, and rain is important to supply the source of drinking water where no man builds reservoirs, pumping plants, and systems of distribution. Of course, underlying all this there is the certainty that were it not for the rain that falls in uninhabited places, there would be no water left for the cities. For in our urban centers we draw upon the surplus of the wilderness, and drink only what they can spare us.

And at what a cost do we thus care for the needs of the citizens who dwell in the teeming centers of population! In the city of Los Angeles, as an instance, we have over a hundred million dollars invested in our waterworks. Across the deserts and the mountains for many miles, the giant aqueduct brings from the wilderness the life-giving fluid for those who dwell in this pleasant place. This marvelous aqueduct, the hydro-electric plants, the reservoirs, settling pools, filters, and pumping plants, together with all the machinery necessary to give the citizens water to drink, totals a fabulous amount of invested money. Not content with this, the city of Los Angeles is now preparing to spend another colossal fortune to bring water from the distant Colorado River into the city, to supply its future needs. All this tremendous fortune is taken out of the income of the tax-weary citizen by added levy, just to get a drink! And the wilderness gets it for nothing! We ought to head a movement to move back to the wilderness!

There is no dearth or want there. No assessments, no new levies or tax collectors, just the providence of the Heavenly Father, established to take care of the wild places where no man is. How humble humanity should be in the face of the mechanism ordained and established for the preservation of life and the continuity of its functioning purpose upon this planet! What an odd spectacle it must be to those who dwell in eternal wisdom, to see puny, finite, earth-bound mortals, whose knowledge does not progress beyond the dim attempts to grasp the *alphabet* of creation, vaunting themselves against the supernal Wisdom that by a gesture and a spoken word set all of this mechanism in motion! Certainly we should pray that we might be kept safe from the sad and childish error of self-esteem. Well, indeed, might we echo the ancient one who said, "What is man, that thou art mindful of him?"

In the course of this series of questions on meteorology, there is introduced, as well, the mystery of winter. The question is phrased in words that perhaps many modern men have pondered. When "the waters are hid as a stone," why is the "face of the deep" frozen? It has been stated by some authorities that water is the major mystery with which science deals today. It was supposed at one time that this common combination of two gases in the universal proportion of two molecules of hydrogen to one molecule of oxygen was a natural composition which never varied. However, the work of the famous Harvard physicist which resulted in the production of what is termed "heavy water" has showed that this was a baseless postulation. This so-called "heavy water" will not support life, and it is theoretically presumed at the present time that to drink a glassful of this strange substance would unquestionably result in the death of the hardy soul who tried it.

It was not an accident of creation that caused water to be formed into the usable shape that sustains life upon this planet. Nothing in this world can live without water in some form or quantity, yet almost nothing is known about it. We know that it is composed of two gases, oxygen and hydrogen. Oxygen is essential to all combustion. Hydrogen is ignited more easily than any other gas. The natural supposition would be that combining these two inflammable substances would result in the production of a highly explosive force, but the contrary is true. When these inflammable substances are combined, they put the fire out! It would be a dangerous experiment to try that method with any other inflammable substances, such as kerosene and gasoline. The experimenter would probably go out before the fire did!

This mysterious substance can be expanded twelve hundred times and called steam. We can then turn this vapor into a stone and call it ice. Once more, we reduce it to a fluid, and never lose a drop of the amount we started with! This mysterious substance will purr with contentment as it grinds our food and lights our homes, or it will roar like a demon when it gets out of control and destroys the homes and cities that it helped to build. Water will give us life one minute, and take it away the next. It is indeed a mysterious factor of the physical universe, and nowhere is its mystery more enhanced than when considered in the light of the thought about its winter conduct, as suggested in this text.

Job is raising the question here, "What is the scientific reason for the strange conduct of ice? Why does it hide the face of the water, when it ought to sink like a stone?" If it did, of course the seas, lakes, and streams would all be frozen from the bottom to the top, and a period of glaciation would ensue. All life would perish from the waters, and the earth would soon become a dismal waste under a fresh encroachment of polar seas. But instead of this, ice floats, and in the winter season life is preserved beneath this strange mantle of stone.

This is an apparent violation of an established law of physics. This law, applied broadly to all the substances of nature is, "Heat expands objects and cold contracts them." Water, however, seems to be a Bolshevik! When it starts to freeze, it first follows this law and begins to contract. If you had the optical apparatus to make this conduct visible, and could watch the water freezing, you would see it losing bulk as the molecules huddled together for warmth. As the temperature dropped dangerously close to the freezing point, the water would lose bulk, becoming smaller and smaller. Within a few degrees of the point where the water will be ice, and because of this law of contraction will necessarily sink like a stone, the cold water goes on a rampage and violates what might be called known law.

Of course, we understand that it is acting upon an unknown law that is peculiar to its own nature. At any rate, an apparent miracle happens. Suddenly the contraction ceases, and in the next few degrees of lowered temperature, the freezing water gains back all of the bulk it has previously lost, plus almost one-third more. Thus the ice floats on the surface, and the life that God made is preserved by this ingenious method from year to year, contrary to what might be called established law.

At other times, the water obeys this law, for when heat is applied to fluid water, it begins to swell and expand until it forms a vapor which we call steam. Decreasing temperature applied to this steam shrinks it back into the normal bulk of water again. But when that shrinking has gone so far that it endangers life in the ponds and streams, these molecules of water become flushed with indignation and, heated by this outrage, puff out their tiny chests and expand to their uttermost capacity, to present this puzzle to Job. Not only to Job, but to the modern man as well, is this conduct of water highly intriguing.

Of course, we presume that Job in his simplicity, would answer the question, "Why does ice float instead of sinking," by the ingenious reply, "Because God made it that way." Can modern man, with all his vaunted learning, find a better answer than this?

Certainly water is beyond the power of man's production and control. With humility Job hung his head and answered in the negative when God said to him, "Canst thou lift up thy voice to the clouds, that abundance of waters may cover thee?" With that same humility, we shake our heads in sorrow and despair when dust storms devastate our terrain today. The reader will perhaps remember that during a trip by the chief executive of the United States through the country devastated by drought, at one station in the Dakotas the president's private car was met by a vast throng of people, displaying placards expressing their sentiments. One placard so impressed the writer that he has never been able to forget it. The horrible, barren landscape, moving off in lots of thousands of tons as it was stirred by the relentless wind, served as a background for a banner which read, "You gave us beer; now give us water." This, alas, the most powerful executive in the civilized world confessed himself unable to do.

Various experimenters have dreamed of the possibility of causing rain. Some men have even claimed to have accomplished this, but when put to the test, their puny efforts availed less than nothing. There is a strong sense of uneasiness stirring the hearts of many of the leaders of the United States even as we write, because of the continuance of these frightful droughts and dust storms, which may perhaps turn fruitful sections of our great nation into a desert as barren as the Sahara or the Gobi. We do know that not many thousands of years ago the famous Gobi desert was a fruitful, productive area, containing magnificent cities and supporting a vast population.

Then something happened that was beyond the power of man to control or direct. It was a simple thing. The direction of the prevailing winds shifted. Then slowly but inexorably, like a marching army from the very portals of hell, sands carried on the bosom of the breeze blotted out city after city, swept over farm after farm, dried up one water course after another, while the brazen heavens were sealed so that no water fell. The people who inhabited those fair cities of the Gobi are long since dead. Archaeologists delve beneath those shifting sands for evidences of their culture and some knowledge of their history. If all could stand today in the witness box of this inquiry and seek to answer this question for Job, their united voices would be one unbroken testimony to the inability of man to control these mighty forces of nature. Four thousand years ago, Job said, "No, Lord, I am dependent upon Providence for rain." Has man a better answer today?

Of course we recognize the fact that there are some things we can do that were beyond the power of Job. In the day of Job, no man had ever dreamed of harnessing lightning to the will of a human driver. So when Job was asked, in the thirty-fifth verse, "Canst thou send lightnings, that they may go, and say unto thee, 'Here we are'?" we may well imagine the stupendous wonder of the ancient patriarch. Who ever dreamed of making a messenger of the lightning in Job's day? Yet in our day, because we have captured some of His thoughts after the Creator, we see in the lightning a common convenience. Sometimes we step into the telegraph office and command the lightnings to carry our words across the continent, and they obey. We step into the same office, and the lightning bears our words beneath the sea, to deliver them to some far-flung island or distant land. Electricity is lightning, and vice versa, and it has become the willing and obedient slave and messenger of man. If the words we entrust to them are of sufficient importance to the sender, we can demand of the lightning a report, and after they bear our words from coast to coast, the lightnings will speed back and say, "Here we are, and we told your message." Or if we are too impatient to wait for the comparatively slow operation of the telegraph, we can take down the receiver of the telephone and speak half way around the globe. There is no time lapse in this method of communication. As fast as we can speak, our words will be borne by the lightning at the speed of light. As we noted in the preceding chapter, it is a very common experience for men on the Atlantic seaboard to call their friends, acquaintances, and business contacts somewhere on the Pacific coast. Within fifteen seconds of the time their call is placed, they hear the answering voice three thousand miles away. But after the lapse of the initial fifteen seconds, distance no longer exists, and the response is as instant as though both parties were in the same room, face to face.

Even more remarkable in the conquest of space is man's ability to broadcast his spoken word over aerial lanes. While the human voice is traveling thirteen feet, the radio will fling it one thousand miles. Around and around the earth the voice of radio goes, so that before a second and a half have elapsed, it is possible for a message to girdle the globe and bring back a reply. Of course, the patriarch Job never dreamed of such marvels as this four thousand years ago. When he was alive, lightning was one of the wildest and most implacable enemies that men possessed. It struck wherever it willed, and man could do nothing but cower in terror before its awful power. In a sense of the word, lightning is still sovereign today, for when it crackles across the inverted dome of the upper atmosphere, men still shudder in fear before its awful power, but from the time that the great Benjamin Franklin flew his historic kite, down to the present hour, men of this marvelous age have been gathering this lightning out of the firmament. They have made of it a homing pigeon which with gentle and faithful alacrity will bear the words of men. What a marvelous Book, that anticipated this triumph of man's ingenuity by some four thousand years or more!

We would recommend to the thoughtful reader a long and careful study of this thirty-eighth chapter of Job. If there were in all the Scripture no other evidence of inspiration and the certainty of revelation, we believe it would be found here. One of the most suggestive of all these questions, and one that may well cause the modern mind to ponder deeply, is found in the thirty-first verse. Here the query is raised, "Canst thou bind the sweet influences of Pleiades, or loose the bands of Orion?" An acquaintance who spent the first forty years of his life in ancient Mesopotamia, the land where Job lived, brought to us some light upon this rather fascinating query. He said that though they are, of course, close together in the sky in that far-away eastern land, the Pleiades and Orion are the constellations which introduce the spring and winter seasons. So this is a pertinent question that God asks of Job, nor can it be answered by any man since Job, including the present generation. When the Pleiades shone in the sky at night, the men of that land knew that spring had come. Note, then, this question carefully, "Canst thou bind the sweet influence of Pleiades?" That is to say, when sap has begun to flow, when the leaf has appeared on the bough, and the tree has put forth her blossoms. when the grass springs forth from the sod, and the rill and the brook begin to sing, is there any human influence which can lock them again in the still bands of winter? In a word, when God begins to make a spring, no man can hinder or retard.

In the same sense of finality, when Orion flamed in the sky of that land, winter had come. How utterly fantastic for man to seek to reply in the affirmative to this question of God, "Canst thou loose the bands of Orion?" No man can loose the bands of winter. When the blossom and the leaf disappear and all the singing waters are locked in the icy manacles of winter, who can hinder God in the progress of the season?

We might say again that this is a humorous suggestion from deity. To Job He said in effect, "Get some experience with little things first, and learn to control the seasons. When you can turn back the winter or the spring which I have begun, then you may have the power to change the weight and authority of my words." There is no modern science that can do so here. There is no man of erudition or power who can bind the influence of the Pleiades, or loose the bands of Orion. This is indeed a striking example of modern science in an ancient Book. In the archaic day of Job, how could he even have asked these questions which twentieth century wisdom cannot answer? Again we reply that in the book of Job, at least, men of old spake as they were moved by the Spirit of God.

Modern Science, Jonah, and the Whale

CHAPTER V

Modern Science, Jonah, and the Whale

IN weighing the evidences for the inspiration of the Bible, there are many lines of investigation that are a delight to the Christian investigator. No single fact that is advanced for the support and comfort of the faith, however, is of more practical value and interest than is the fact of the poverty of the critic. Almost two thousand years of culture and learning have passed since the manuscripts of the Bible were completed. Some four thousand years have gone by since the record was first begun. In those multiplied centuries the wisdom of man has increased to an astounding degree. Yet when men today draw upon that vast body of new knowledge for help in their criticism of the Scripture, they receive cold comfort indeed.

We have frequently pondered upon the interesting fact that after these centuries of criticism and study, the enemy of the Bible is restricted to not more than five or six pseudo-scientific arguments against its integrity. We frequently hear the critics say that there are scores of scientific errors in the Bible. When challenged to enumerate a few of these scores, they invariably name, at the most, five or six possible errors. Upon investigation even these fade away and leave the Bible utterly unchallenged in its claim to inspiration. Over and over, these five or six objections are reiterated, and they are the sole stock in trade of the infidel. These stock objections will be the subject of the ensuing chapters. In this section of our writings, we shall show beyond question that these so-called weaknesses of the Bible constitute one of its strongest features.

Among these few available arguments that are offered against the doctrine of the scientific accuracy of the Bible, the one most frequently advanced by the superficial critic is the modern objection to the story of Jonah and the whale. Cheap witticism has labeled this account, "the greatest fish story in history." Many men who have never studied the narrative claim that it is the most outstanding weakness of the entire Bible. Infidelity has long laughed at this strange record, has derided its accuracy and questioned its probability, but has never disproved the historicity of the affair. Undaunted by the light laughter of empty objections, the man of intelligence proceeds to investigate and find the truth of the matter by research.

The book of Jonah consists of four chapters, with a total number of only forty-eight verses. It can be read easily in less than five minutes by the average reader. Yet in many parts of America we have asked audiences how many of them have read this short book through at one sitting. One never finds that more than ten per cent of any crowd has ever done so! The most widely discussed book in the Bible, and not ten per cent of the Christian populace ever invested five minutes to see what the argument was about!

The entire book of Jonah would be accepted even by the modern critics, if we would expurgate two verses from its contents. The rest of the book is admittedly a valuable historic document, were it not "ruined" by the introduction of these two verses. The first of these disputed passages is the last verse of the first chapter, and the other one is the last verse of the second chapter.

The reader will recall how the first chapter of the book of Jonah recounts the fact that God's wrath was kindled against Nineveh, because of its outstanding sin. God, Who is ever gracious and slow to anger, sent a message to the prophet Jonah, instructing him to proceed to Nineveh. He was to bear the message of a coming destruction of the city with all of its inhabitants, unless they repented and turned from their sin. Instead of going to Nineveh, however, Jonah found a ship that was going to Tarshish, and fled from the direction of Nineveh as fast as he could travel. The residence of the prophet was in Gath-hepher, and when he started for Tarshish, it was directly opposite to the direction of Nineveh. But as Jonah was seeking to flee from God's appointed task, a mighty storm arose, threatening the very safety of the ship in which the prophet sailed. When the men of the ship learned that this storm came upon them because of Jonah, at his own behest they threw him overboard. To save their own lives, they jeopardized his.

This resumé brings us to the first disputed verse, which is given in these simple words: "Now the Lord had prepared a great fish to swallow up Jonah. And Jonah was in the belly of the fish three days and three nights."

The second disputed verse is in the second chapter. The first verse of this chapter is certainly admissible: "Then Jonah prayed unto the Lord his God out of the fish's belly." We are quite sure no intelligent person would find fault with that statement. The amazing thing is that the obstinate prophet waited three days to begin. Had one of us been swallowed by that fish, in less than three minutes the Lord would have heard our cry, "Let me out; I want to go to Nineveh!" So even the most rabid critic does not question the statement that Jonah prayed from the depths of this sea monster. Any man in Jonah's case would have cried out to God.

The first nine verses of the chapter, then, deal with the prayer of Jonah, and the tenth and final verse is the disputed record. This statement is made in these simple words, "And the Lord spake unto the fish, and it cast out Jonah upon the dry land." Without any attempt at textual comment, we have simply quoted these verses from the authorized edition of the English Bible, as this edition is familiar to more people than any other. This, then, is the story at which infidelity has laughed for centuries. We repeat, however, that this is an account which infidelity has never disproved.

The prophet Jonah is an interesting character. The school of higher criticism, denying all miraculous elements in God's dealings with men, has refused to accept the tale of the fish. If we would delete these two verses containing the record of the miracle, they would find the book acceptable to their fancy. However, it has never been profitable in any generation for men to alter the written records of God's Word to harmonize with the demands of the so-called scholarship of that generation. We are under the necessity of accepting the Book just as God wrote it, and our knowledge must be brought into harmony with His revelation.

Not willing to bow before the higher wisdom of the Holy Spirit, the critics have sought to deny the historical existence of an actual Jonah. They have said that he was a legendary hero of Jewish folk-lore and fable, as was Hercules among the Greeks. The contrary, however, is the truth. Jonah is as historical a character as was Napoleon Bonaparte or Rameses the Second. They may readily be established by an appeal to a reliable book of pure history. In all the historical records of any people, there are none that are superior to the books of the Kings, which records were kept by the Hebrew people under the direction of God's Spirit. The recent advancement of archaeological learning, if it has done nothing else, has established the credibility of these Scriptures.

In Second Kings, the fourteenth chapter, there is a historical reference to the prophet Jonah that authenticates this character and gives him an established background. In this passage of Scripture the father of Jonah is named, thus giving his genealogy. The place of his residence is told. We also learn the name of the king who ruled when Jonah was alive. History further attests that some of his prophecies were fulfilled in the reign of that king. So from this historical reference we see that Jonah was a real person.

To complete the case and make the evidence perfect, there is one other source of testimony to the reality of Jonah that cannot be set aside. We refer to the conclusive testimony of the Lord Jesus Christ. When the Son of God speaks upon any subject, that testimony is and should be conclusive. In the days of His flesh He was betrayed in the house of His friends by one of His followers. Today He has many so-called friends who by their infidelity and unbelief re-enact the drama of Judas. But believing friend and disbelieving enemy alike are united in their praise of His character. Not even His bitterest enemies impugn His veracity or question the honesty of His statements.

So it is with a great deal of assurance that we turn to Christ's testimony concerning the historicity of this man Jonah. In the course of His ministry among men, Jesus made two references to Jonah as a historical character. In one He gives the experience of Jonah as a type of His own burial and resurrection. When the scribes and Pharisees demanded of Him proof of His deity, they asked that this proof be given in the form of a sign. Jesus replied to their demand, "A wicked and adulterous generation seek after a sign. There shall no sign be given you, save the sign of the prophet Jonah. As Jonah was three days and three nights in the belly of the sea monster, so must the Son of Man be three days and three nights in the depths of the earth." These two experiences are interdependent and equally historical. Since the resurrection of Jesus Christ is established upon the most unquestioned evidence, and since the experience of Jonah is as real as was the resurrection of Jesus, this testimony of the Saviour is of peculiar and striking force.

The second reference that Jesus made to the historicity of Jonah was a citation of the repentance of Nineveh. As Jesus was teaching and preaching in the course of His ministry, He met with considerable hardness of heart, and in some cases, with outright rejection. On one of these occasions our Lord said, "The men of Nineveh shall rise up in judgment against this generation and shall condemn it, because they repented in the presence of Jonah; but behold, a greater than Jonah is here." We have this authority of Jesus for saying that Jonah as a character is as truly historical as is the person of Jesus Himself.

One of the fascinating things in the writings of Jonah is the manner in which his character is displayed in this very brief section of his autobiography. Jonah is perhaps one of the most honest writers in literature, for he writes boldly and bluntly of his own faults. He tells of his stubbornness as he set his own judgment against the command of God. He tells without apology of the waywardness of his conduct as he fled from the call of God. But with a rare dependence, he gives no explanation and offers no excuse. He is content to say with charming simplicity just what he did, and offers no motive for his conduct.

This course of procedure has laid the prophet open to another assault on the part of the critics. Jonah seems to have been the first foreign missionary. He was called of God to bring a warning of the consequence of sin to a foreign people. With that warning he was to deliver also an offer of redemption and mercy if they would turn to God and repent. This service he refused at first. Later, however, repenting of his refusal, he returned and preached to this nation with tremendous effect. So widespread was the revival that resulted from Jonah's preaching, that every soul in the kingdom was converted, from the king on his throne down to the humblest subject in the streets. Even the animals were garbed in the habiliments of mourning and penitence, as the grace of God manifested itself in the sorrow of the repentant sinners.

Now in this account of Jonah's refusal to serve and in his attempted flight to Tarshish, the higher critic has found much comfort. One of the favorite arguments of the modernistic school is the baseless assertion that the revelation of God in the Old and New Testaments constitutes an evolution of the idea of God. They falsely state that beginning with a God of restricted authority Who was merely a tribal deity, men gradually evolved the idea of a God Who is the universal Father of humanity. Of course, any honest student reading the Scripture with anything more than casual interest will realize that this theory is not borne out by the text.

In the first place, it is nowhere stated in the Old Testament that God was a tribal deity. In fact, the first revelation of God in the Scripture is the highest revelation that the Bible contains. The first chapter of Genesis opens with the record of an omnipotent, omniscient Deity, Who by His spoken word created the heavens and the earth, and all things therein. There is certainly nothing tribal in the picture of the Creator that Moses draws in the first book of the Bible.

We further see that this God Who is the Creator is a beneficent and kindly deity. In those same early writings we find Him walking and talking in Eden's garden with the creatures whom He has created. That picture of a loving God in intimate personal communion with His creatures is never equalled, even in Holy Writ, until Jesus Christ comes saying, "And when ye pray, say, Father." The Saviour, however, was careful to state that God is only the Father of those who love and serve Him. To the enemies of God's message, Jesus said, "Ye are the children of your father, the devil, and the works of your father ye will do."

So the conclusions of higher criticism are baseless here. Their premise is also faulty. There is no evolution of the idea of God, nor does the Bible anywhere teach the universal fatherhood of God!

One of the strongest arguments of the critical school, however, for their fallacious philosophy, has been the conduct of Jonah. When God called him for one specific service, he fled from the call of God and headed for Tarshish. The higher critic has sought to show that Jonah believed that God's power was restricted to Palestine. So if he got beyond the confines of Palestine, his God could not reach him.

The most cursory examination of Jonah's creed, however, will show that such is far from the truth. The unbeliever, infidel, atheist, or higher critic can find no comfort in this record, for his weird idea of Jonah's belief in God. For Jonah believed in a God Who was omnipotent and universal. If you will read again the first chapter of this noted book, you will find that while the storm was raging at its height, Jonah slept in peaceful security in the heart of the ship. When the captain wakened him and said, "Who art thou?" Jonah's reply contained his creed.

Hear again these marvelous words, "I am a Hebrew; and I fear *the God of heaven, which hath made the sea and the dry land.*" Is that a tribal deity? Is that a description of a God Whose power was circumscribed by the geographical limits of Palestine? Jonah recognized the universal nature of the Creator, and knew that he could not journey beyond His reach.

The question arises then, "Why did Jonah flee toward Tarshish, if he was not striving to get out of the reach of God? Why did he take this ship that would bear him away from Nineveh?"

Let us remember that Jonah, like all the prophets of Israel, was intensely patriotic. He loved his own nation and people, and the most bitterly hated enemy possessed by Israel at this period was Nineveh. When the Word of God came to Jonah saying that He would destroy Nineveh unless they repented, Jonah, in the fervor of his patriotic heart, said, "That suits me. If God will wipe out Nineveh, that will constitute a patriotic victory for Israel, and I will get as far away from Nineveh as I can."

In other words, Jonah was an ordinary human with the passions, the interests, and the psychology of any modern man. This same instinct of patriotism was manifested in some of the most cultivated Christian men of the twentieth century when the United States of America entered the World War. Men who had radiated love, and had talked about the international brotherhood of man, began to curse the Germans and damn the Kaiser, only because that race had become this nation's enemy! Jonah thought and reasoned and acted exactly as a modern would do in the same circumstances.

The element of the supernatural entered into the account of Jonah's experience *before the introduction of the fish that swallowed him.* God followed Jonah from the time of the prophet's defection until he returned in submission and humility. First of all, He followed Jonah with a storm, for Jonah testified that the storm came upon the ship because of him. So little did Jonah fear the effects of that storm, reposing as he did in the confidence of the keeping care of God, that God followed Jonah again in the call of the captain of the vessel. The prophet was further pursued by the intention of God when, as the men cast their lots, the lot fell upon Jonah. When he was cast over the side of the ship, the supernatural element of the story continues with the very simple statement that God had *prepared* a great fish to be the temporary host of Jonah.

Then this brings us to the account of the fish. We suppose that it is only natural that every man will investigate any questioned case from the viewpoint of his own preconceived prejudice. It might be argued that we were not able to make a fair examination of the story of Jonah because we came to the study of the account with a strong belief that it was true.

If this is so, it is because we have previously read the testimony of Jesus Christ, Whose Word we unhesitatingly accept upon any question of which He speaks. Even without the testimony of Jesus, we would be inclined to believe the story of Jonah is true, because the infidel and the atheist are united in denying it! We confess to a mental revulsion against such company, and almost automatically accept what they reject. We have noticed in these years of scientific study that atheism and infidelity never investigate or conduct research except under the prejudice of unbelief. Whenever an atheist starts out to investigate or study a matter with an absolutely closed mind, the whole attempt revolves itself into an effort to disprove the subject he is investigating. The infidel is almost as bad.

There is, however, no counter explanation to this account of the strange experience of Jonah that will satisfy the inquiring mind if we rule out the supernatural. One critic says that Jonah had a bad nightmare and that when he awakened, he wrote his dream. Another doubter says that the entire book of Jonah is a simple fabrication, that none of the incidents are historical. One weird near-thinker states that when Jonah was cast overboard from the ship, he was picked up by a vessel following. The second ship had as a figurehead the image of a fish, so when the men in the first ship saw the rescue of Jonah by this following ship, they said that he had been swallowed by a monster of the deep! But the Bible simply and literally states that a sea monster *that God had prepared* swallowed Jonah.

We call your attention now to the phrase, "that God prepared." The whole argument must turn upon these words. The question is raised, "Is God able to prepare a fish that would accommodate a man and keep him alive for as long as seventy-two hours?" If God cannot do this, then He is indeed tremendously inferior to man. Recently a company of finite men, who had some small engineering skill, built an iron fish. Twenty men entered this iron fish and remained under water for twelve days and twelve nights. At the end of that time they came to the surface again to replenish their supplies of food and oxygen. The iron fish sent them forth on the dry land for a period of relaxation. Again twenty men entered this iron fish and descended into the deep. Of course, they called this man-made fish a submarine, and nobody doubted the ability of men of mechanical and mental ingenuity to construct such a fish. They are common today.

How weird it seems to us who think things through, that men see the evidences of man's power to work these so-called miracles, and will yet deny the same degree of power to God!

Again we see that God prepared other things besides the fish. In the story of Jonah there was a vine that was prepared; there was a worm that was specifically sent. There was a strong east wind that blew at an untimely season. The God Who made the heavens and the earth prepared a fish, a worm, and a vine.

Some years ago, when we were excavating some of those famous shell mounds of the southern area, we had the pleasure of fellowship with an unusually brilliant man of science. This man was a keen, intelligent thinker, not related in any sense to the household of faith. During the steamy heat of the mid-day, when it was impossible for men to work with any comfort whatever, we lolled around in the shade of the semi-tropical verdure and took what ease the weather would permit. In those times of friendly converse we discussed almost everything in which we had mutual interest. One day the conversation turned upon the Bible. In some curiosity, the writer said to his fellow-archaeologist, "How is it that a man of your mental attainments has never become a Christian?"

Very earnestly he replied, "It seems to me that Christianity must stand or fall with the Bible. I have never become a Christian, beautiful and attractive as Christianity is to me, because I cannot accept the Bible as the infallibly inspired Word of God that you Christians claim it to be."

Finding that we had the same sense of value as to the foundational need of the Scripture, the writer replied, "I agree with you, Bob. Jesus Christ and the Bible must stand or fall together. But upon the basis of evidence, and after long years of study and thought, I do receive the Bible as the inspired Word of God. Why do you not receive it that way?"

"Because I cannot accept *any* of the Bible *unless I take it all!*"

"Check again. What part of the Bible do you not receive? I believe it all."

"Well, for one thing, I cannot believe that old fish story about Jonah and the whale."

We looked at him in surprise for a moment, and then said, "Is it possible that a man who knows as much about marine biology as you know, does not appreciate how credible and probable that entire account may be?"

The man sat up as though he had been stabbed with a thorn. Gripping our arm with some intensity, he said, "Now, listen! I do not say to you, 'Prove that that thing happened.' I know that that would be practically impossible. It is also unnecessary. But I do say to you that *if you can prove that it is reasonably and scientifically probable*, that's all I will ask. For if you demonstrate to me that this thing *could* have happened, I will accept the story as truth, on the basis that it is in the Bible."

That is clear thinking. This is also the limit of the mental cooperation we ask of those who read these pages. Of course, we cannot demonstrate on present-day testimony that the experience of Jonah was exactly as it was written in his book. We were not there. However, we can show from the records of science that it is highly probable, and that the thing *could* have happened exactly as Jonah recounted his experience. For when we bring to light the evidence of modern scientific research upon the record of Jonah, that record is shown as being reasonable in the light of present evidence.

The only objection of the infidel that we have ever read is that there is no whale that has a throat large enough to swallow a man. It is sometimes difficult to understand how the *whale* crept into this story. The Scripture in the original languages nowhere says that Jonah's host was a whale. In the book of Jonah in the Hebrew language, the word there translated "fish" is the Hebrew word "dag". This word appears in the Old Testament nineteen times, and is translated on each occasion "fish." We know, of course, that the whale is not a fish, so if the Scripture in the Hebrew text says that a fish swallowed Jonah, the whale is ruled out at once. The whale is a mammal. It follows the order of viviparous birth. It suckles its young and is a warm-blooded animal. It would be scientifically incorrect to speak of the whale as a fish.

In the King James version of the New Testament there is an incorrect translation that makes this fish appear as a whale. Jesus did not say that Jonah was three days and three nights in the whale's belly. The translators, in dealing with this passage in the original Greek, used the word "whale" because it was the only sea creature they knew that was big enough to suit them. The word, however, is "ketos"—and simply means a monster of the deep. The

Hebrew word for whale is "tannin". The Old Testament Scripture says that Jonah was swallowed by a great "dag". The New Testament says that he was picked up by a "ketos", and nowhere does the original writing say that this was a whale.

The Old and New Testament both agree, however, that a fish or a monster of the deep received Jonah into its capacious maw, where he resided for three days and three nights. But let us suppose that the creature of the deep was in very fact a whale. It would still be reasonable and scientifically demonstrable that *a whale could have swallowed Jonah!*

The whales constitute the genus cetacea. This genus is divided into two general groups, the first of which is composed of all the whales that are known as Denticete. These are the whales, as their name suggests, that are armed with teeth. Most of this variety do not have teeth on both jaws, but they have several strong, well-defined teeth in their lower jaw which fit into sockets in the upper jaw. They use these teeth for tearing loose their food and crushing squids and preparing them for the first steps of digestion. The sperm whale, for instance, which is a monster that often reaches a length of sixty and sixty-five feet, has forty-four teeth in the lower jaw, but has only the sockets in the upper jaw. This whale has an extremely small throat. He chews his food and crushes it. It is evident at once that this whale could not have swallowed Jonah, because of his custom of chewing, and the restricted area of the esophagus. Presumably this type of whale, which has been the chief object of commercial pursuit, gave rise to the current belief that NO whale could swallow Jonah.

There is another whale of this same type, the Denticete, known as the "bottle-nosed" or "beaked" whale. Its scientific name is Tiphiide. This is a small whale, not over thirty feet long. Although this whale is only half the size of the sperm whale, it has a throat big enough to swallow a man. However, we exclude this whale from being Jonah's host, because it also is armed with teeth and chews its food.

We do not desire to make this study technical, and so we will pass on to say that the other type of whale is known as the Mysticete. This group is composed of the whales that have no teeth. In place of teeth they are equipped with whale bone plates, called balaena. These plates form the sieve through which the food of the whale is strained. These plates vary from eighteen inches in length to twelve feet in some cases. One particular whale of the order Mysticete has plates that are eighteen inches in width at the juncture with the jaw. They taper down to about the width of the hand and become finally attenuated, something after the order of the straws in a whisk-broom. The ends of the upper and lower balaena join in the center of the mouth, forming a sieve through which the food is strained, as stated above.

This group of whales has a curious habit of feeding. They open their mouths, submerge their lower jaws, and rush through the water at a terrific speed. When one of them thus feeding has filled his gigantic mouth, he closes his jaws and curls back his lips. By a muscular pressure of the tongue he forces the water out of his mouth, straining it through his balaena, or plates. When the water is all excluded, the whale swallows whatever is left in his mouth. Some of these creatures are armed with these plates to the number of three hundred on each side. The balaena is the source of the whalebone of trade. These whales migrate from sea to sea, and since all seas connect somewhere, they may be found in their migrations and wanderings in strange, out-of the-way places.

It is in this order of whale that the very largest types are found. They form a fascinating field of study. For instance, there is that variety called the Megaptera Medosa, or "humpbacked" whales. They are weird looking as they pass in the sea, being about fifty feet in length, with their head forming fully one-third of their entire length. They have a low, thick dorsal fin which adds to their humpbacked appearance. The pectoral fins are fifteen feet long, and as they speed through the water, these pectorals assume the appearance of wings. They are covered with rows of longitudinal ridges like a rib thread automobile tire. They feed on anything that floats on the surface of the sea.

The largest whale known is the Balaenoptera Musculus, commonly called the "sulphur bottom", belonging to the variety called fin-back. One of them has been measured that was ninety-five feet and six inches in length, while the average length would be in the neighborhood of seventy-six feet. They also are armed with longitudinal ridges. From sixty to ninety protuberant ridges of blubber line them for their entire length. This particular type of whale would have no difficulty whatever in accommodating a man. As an evidence of the size these great animals reach, we quote here an expert, Charles Bell Emerson, who replies to a query by saying:

> "The last account that I have of a big haul was that of the Norwegian whaler, N. T. Nielson Alonso. She was covered from stem to stern with layers of congealed grease, and gave off that peculiar odor of whale oil that you can smell a mile or more; she arrived in Sydney, Australia, on February 29th, from the Ross Sea, as she had to have bunker coal before proceeding to Larvik, Norway.
>
> "Unusually favorable conditions prevailed all the time during the four months' cruise, and the vessel's tanks were full of whale oil to their full capacity.
>
> "And it is recorded that fifty-seven thousand (57,000) barrels of oil were secured on that voyage. This is valued at about $1,330,000.

"There is a record of a sulphur-bottom whale 95 feet in length and having a weight of 147 tons — 294,000 pounds. This specimen, captured off the west coast of North America, is the largest whale of which there is authentic record; this would mean that this one was the largest animal ever known to man, up to date.

"The one that went ashore was big enough so that a 75-ton locomotive crane was unable to lift it out of the entrance to the Panama Canal, so it was towed 12 miles out to sea, and Navy aeroplanes dropped two 160-pound bombs and blew it to pieces."

The whale's stomach is complex, having from four to six chambers or compartments, in any one of which a small colony of men could be readily accommodated.

We have records that show the whale has proved itself host to various living creatures. The whale is an air breathing mammal and cannot live without oxygen. This oxygen it has to get somewhere above the water. As the whale has no gills, it can only submerge as long as its air supply will allow. So all whales have in their heads a wonderful air storage chamber. The chamber is an enlargement of the nasal sinus, and in a very large whale, this strange tank, or compartment, would measure fourteen feet long by seven feet high, and seven feet wide.

Dr. Ransome Harvey recounts that a friend of his, weighing two hundred pounds, climbed from the mouth of a dead whale into this chamber. If the whale takes into its mouth any object too big to swallow, it thrusts it up into this air chamber. If it finds that it has a large object in its head, it swims to the nearest land, lies in shallow water, and ejects it.

Recently in the "Cleveland Plain Dealer" was an article quoting Dr. Ransome Harvey, who says that a dog was lost overboard from a whaler. It was found in the head of the whale six days later alive, and none the worse for its unnatural journey. This quotation from the "Cleveland Plain Dealer" was recently copied by the "Sunday School Times" and caused a great deal of comment.

At any rate it may easily be seen that a man would have no difficulty remaining alive for three days and three nights in an air chamber as extensive as this, containing 686 cubic feet of space.

But let us not forget our original proposition that it may not have been and probably was not a whale. There are sharks that swim the sea that would come under the restricted meaning of the Hebrew word "dag", for these sharks are fish.

The late Dr. A. C. Dixon stated that in a museum at Beirut, there is the head of a shark big enough to swallow the largest man that history records. Dr. Dixon also recounts instances where the white shark of the Mediterranean was known to have swallowed a whole horse. Another one of these monsters of the deep swallowed a reindeer, minus only its horns. In another Mediterranean white shark upon its capture investigators found a whole sea cow, about the size of an ox.

There is a ferocious and voracious shark called the Somnilosis Microcephalous, also known as the "sleeper shark". While it is small, seldom getting more than twenty feet in length, it is the swiftest and most ferocious shark extant. It is known to attack the largest whale and to bite hunks of blubber from this huge mammal until the victim succumbs in death. This shark could have swallowed Jonah, but the difficulty is that it would probably have bitten him into at least two sections.

So we come to the point of this entire discussion. Is there any creature that swims the deep sea whose natural feeding habits and whose entire morphology would make him a logical host for Jonah? As far as we know, there is only one, but we are happy to state that there is one. This is a shark which is known as the Rhinodon Typicus. It is called variously the "bone-shark", the "Indo-Pacific shark", and the "whale-shark", by which latter name it is most commonly known. Recently off the coast of Florida a specimen was captured and exhibited about the country and finally sent to the Smithsonian Institute. This was a comparatively small specimen, being thirty-six feet in length.

This shark gets its common name, the "whale-shark", from the fact that its oral cavity is similar to the structure found in the whale. Sometimes it reaches the length of fifty feet; and one account tells of the largest specimen captured, seventy feet in length. This shark, having no teeth, feeds like the whale, straining its food through great plates in its mouth. It has a capacious maw and could readily swallow a man. Indeed, we have collected many instances where this very thing has occurred. Out of these multiplied occasions we will consider just three. The first record comes to us from the Hawaiian Islands, in whose shark-infested waters the Rhinodon is a common visitor. During a recent visit to the Islands, we saw that a certain soldier from Schofield Barracks, on the Island of Oahu, was reported missing without leave. Thirty days after the man disappeared, a party of Japanese fishermen set out from Hilo to spread their nets, and were chagrined to find a Rhinodon basking on the surface in the vicinity where they desired to spread their nets.

The feeding habits of these great fish are interesting, but fatal to the nets of a fisherman. The shark will bask on the surface of the sea apparently asleep, until assailed by hunger. Then utterly without warning it will open its capacious maw, and with its eyes closed will charge at full speed through the water, engulfing whatever may be floating near the surface.

With a weight of many tons, and a velocity

that makes that weight irresistible, woe to the flimsy nets that meet this charging monster! So fishermen never spread their nets when the Rhinodon is in the region. But the flesh of the shark is used for fertilizer on some of the plantations, and a cent a pound is the reward of the men who capture one.

So the fishermen put back to the port, and procured their harpoons and a high-powered rifle. Quietly approaching the basking creature, they succeeded in their purpose and captured it without much difficulty, and towed the body to the beach. There they cut it open to examine the contents of the stomach, and found therein the skeleton of a six-foot male human being. After thirty days in this weird sepulchre, there was naught left but the bones of the frame, *but every bone was undamaged and undisturbed,* thus evidencing the fact that the man had been swallowed whole. Indeed, as this shark has the balaena common to the whales, in place of the teeth usual to the sharks, it cannot bite or chew, and must swallow whatever it takes into its mouth in one entire piece.

The sad remains of what once had been a man were identified as the missing soldier, and the mystery of his case was thus cleared up to the satisfaction of the authorities. After thirty days there was no possible chance that a man in such condition could survive; this is merely recorded here to establish the fact that the

Rhinodon Typicus does on occasion swallow human beings without harm to them in the process.

That such experiences are more common than is generally believed, may be seen from the clipping taken from the current press. We reproduce the news item in its entirety, having taken pains to prove the accuracy of the report.

FISHERMEN FIND BODY OF MISSING MERCHANT INSIDE GIANT SHARK

Honolulu, T. H., Sept 2 — (By United Press) —Mystery surrounding the disappearance several days ago of Sadao Nakatus, Honolulu merchant, was cleared up Wednesday when fishermen found his body inside a huge shark which they caught off Barber's point.

Identification of the body was through dental work.

Nakatus and another merchant, Minoru Kanagawa, set out last Sunday in a skiff on a fishing expedition. When they failed to return, the destroyer Gamble and the minesweeper Tanager VI began a search for them. Airplanes also joined in the search. The merchant's overturned skiff was found thirty miles off the point, but no trace of either man was found.

Three fisherman caught two sharks in the vicinity of the point Wednesday, brought them ashore, cut them open, and inside of one they found the body of Nakatus.

Two naval aviators who joined the search risked their lives in the shark-infested waters when a plane made a forced landing sixty miles from Honolulu.

The plane, piloted by Lieut. W. L. Rees, rode the seas until the destroyer arrived to take it in tow.

The tragic conclusion of this episode is explained by the phrase, "several days ago." The question that must be settled in the light of this present inquiry is, "What would become of a man who was in this dangerous predicament for just three days and nights?" Once more we have a recent event that will shed some light on the problem.

Some time ago, a magazine devoted to current events contained an account of an English sailor who was swallowed by a gigantic Rhinodon in the English Channel. Briefly, the account stated that in the attempt to harpoon one of these monstrous sharks this sailor fell overboard, and before he could be picked up again, the shark, feeding, turned and engulfed him. His horrified friends made so much outcry that they frightened the fish, and it sounded and disappeared.

The entire trawler fleet put out to hunt the fish down, and forty-eight hours after the accident occurred, the fish was sighted and slain with a one-pound deck gun. The winches on the trawlers were too light to haul up the body of the mighty denizen of the deep, so they towed the carcass to the shore and opened it, to give the body of their friend Christian burial. But when the shark was opened, they were amazed to find the man unconscious but alive! He was rushed to the hospital, where he was found to be suffering from shock alone, and a few hours later was discharged as being physically fit. The account concluded by saying that the man was on exhibit in a London Museum at a shilling admittance fee, being advertised as "The Jonah of the Twentieth Century."

We corresponded with our representatives in London, and shortly afterward received corroboration of this incident, and last year had the privilege of meeting this man in person. His physical appearance was odd, in that his entire body was devoid of hair, and odd patches of a yellowish-brown color covered his entire skin.

For two days and nights he lived in a monster of the deep. And this without any special providential care expressly stated, or even implied. Does it seem reasonable to concede that if a man in the ordinary course of nature can exist for two days and nights inside a marine monster, a prophet of God under His direct care and protection could stand the experience a day and a night longer?

The summary of the matter is this: There are creatures which swim the seas which could in the very course of their nature be hosts to a man like Jonah.

The heart of the matter, however, is this statement from the Book, that God had *prepared* a fish. It is impossible to state whether

God prepared this fish in the natural order of generation and birth or whether this was a special creature.

So the purpose of this demonstration is to show that the account is reasonable. It could have happened. As the intelligent thinker suggested, if it could have happened, and the Scripture says it did happen, upon the authority of Jesus Christ and the weight of attested reason, let us acknowledge the truth of this account.

Modern Science and the Ark of Noah

CHAPTER VI

Modern Science and the Ark of Noah

PERHAPS we should call this chapter "Ignorance and the Ark", for like so many other so-called scientific objections to the truth of God's Word, the arguments that are directed against the record of the ark spring out of ignorance. On this, as upon all other Scriptural subjects, the person who challenges the inspiration and truth of the Bible succeeds magnificently in just one particular. That is, he advertises a boundless and abounding personal ignorance of the subject upon which he speaks. We have often observed that objections made to the Biblical account of Noah's ark are never made from the standpoint of knowledge, but from the viewpoint of misunderstanding.

Many years ago, we spent part of our childhood in a small town, which had its local infidel, as did most such centers of residence. It was his constant boast that he was too "educated" to believe the Bible, and after "thorough" study, he had rejected it entirely. One day, in an informal discussion, this wise unbeliever hung himself, as calves are said to do when they have plenty of rope! Turning to the teacher who had for an hour confounded him in every point, the exasperated infidel asked, "Do you believe the story of the ark that Noah built?"

The teacher replied, "I certainly do."

A foxy gleam lit the eye of the infidel.

"Tell me," he said, "How long was the ark?"

"Three hundred cubits long, fifty wide, and thirty high."

"It must have weighed several hundred pounds?" the questioner slyly continued.

"Certainly," replied the victim, "It probably weighed several hundred tons!"

"Then," cried the infidel in unholy, gleeful triumph, "if the Bible is true, as you claim it is, *how could those two priests in Exodus pick up the ark and carry it across the Red Sea?*"

It is not too much to say that this is a typical attitude. The critic who wisely discourses on the scientific impossibility of the story of the ark, hardly knows that there was an Ark of the Covenant, as well as the ark of the deluge! No believer ever need fear what science may say about the ark of Noah, for science has said all it can say here, and its statements substantiate the account of that ark as the record is given in the Book of Genesis.

In certain learned circles, it is considered quite witty to poke fun at "Mr. Noah's houseboat." Even the brilliant Mr. Brisbane, writing his column for the newspaper syndicate which broadcasts his thoughts widely, has a try at the game. Speaking of the giant reptiles called dinosaurs, which roamed the earth ages ago, Mr. Brisbane says that they were ninety feet long and weighed a hundred tons. (This is, no doubt, true.) Mr. Brisbane's comment is that "Noah must have been crowded in the ark with two of these." His honesty of intent is evidenced, when he later says they roamed the earth five hundred million years ago. Does Mr. Brisbane honestly believe it is five hundred million years since Noah built the ark? Of course not; he holds that these animals were all extinct ages before Noah lived, but any slim chance to poke fun of God's Book must not be missed.

The story of the ark has frequently been picked out as a weak point in the Bible's claim to full and absolute inspiration. However, the critics may as well give up hope; there are no weak points in the Book. Every section of the Scripture that is or has ever been under fire has emerged from the crucible secure for all time. Especially is this so when the point has been a scientific one.

Some time ago we were delivering a series of addresses in a small town in Texas, and we came into violent contact with a local infidel and agnostic who had gained a good deal of pseudo-scientific information. Vain speculation and impossible, wild guesses all were accepted by him without effort. He was somewhat feared locally because of a superficial knowledge of scientific language. We locked horns many times, until finally he said, "I don't want to talk to you any more; you talk to me as though I were an ignorant fool!" We replied, "That is the finest case of self-analysis I ever saw!" Although he was angry for a while, he came back to see the "wherein" and "whyfor." To open the issue, he challenged the truth and historicity of the account of the flood.

He began by saying, "Now take that ridiculous story of the ark. You certainly can't claim that story is scientifically possible."

"Certainly it is," we replied. "What's wrong with it scientifically?"

"Just this," he answered, "it was utterly impossible for Noah to get two animals of every kind into an ark the size of the one he built."

"Let's examine your argument," we replied. "How many different kinds of animals are there?"

He looked at us for several seconds with a blank expression, and then said, "Well, how many kinds are there?"

"Oh, no," we said, "this is your argument; you go ahead and make it."

After some attempt to evade, he said, "Well, I don't know how many kinds of animals there are, but I will soon find out."

Upon this note he departed. When we saw him again later in the day, he cried out in triumph, "I know now how many kinds of animals there are!"

"All right," we said, "how many kinds are there?"

He said, "There are one million different kinds."

Now, of course he was wrong. His figures were highly inaccurate. But since it was his argument and not ours, we let him make it. So we contented ourselves by replying, "What is the argument now?"

He answered, "It was utterly impossible for Noah to get two million animals into an ark the size of the one he built."

"But," we said, "he didn't have to. Out of all the living creatures known to the science of biology, sixty per cent of them live in the water, and a flood wouldn't hurt them."

"Even at that", he answered, "forty per cent of two million animals is a whale of a lot."

"You are forgetting," we retorted, "that out of the forty per cent that live on the dry land, seventy out of every one hundred are insects, which do not take up much room."

Upon which he got somewhat excited, and raised his voice to shout, "But you have to admit that two elephants will take up a lot of room!"

Whereupon we smiled and said, "But think of all the insects the size of fleas which could be parked on two elephants, all of them counting and yet not detracting much from the available space."

In some exasperation he said, "Well, no matter how you try to whittle it down, even ten per cent of two million animals could not possibly get in an ark the size of the one that Noah built."

"All right", we said, "How big was the ark?"

He replied, "What do you mean, 'How big was it?' "

We said, "Exactly that. How big was the ark?"

After considerable embarrassed silence, he was forced to admit that he did not know. He did not know whether the ark was ten miles long by five miles wide or whether it was ten feet long by twenty feet wide. We concluded this phase of our discussion by saying, "Now do you see why we talk to you the way you claim we do? What an intelligent argument is this! Here is a totally unknown number of animals, and here is a boat of absolutely unknown size. Yet you claim it is scientifically impossible to get an unknown number of animals into a boat of an unknown size!"

By this time he was quite wroth, and departed saying, "I will find out how big the ark was!"

We had the last word, however, by calling after him, "You should have found out before you rejected the story."

The next day he came in grim determination to say, "Now I know how big the ark was."

"All right," we answered, "how big was it?"

He said, "It was three hundred cubits long by fifty cubits wide and thirty cubits high."

"Could that hold two of every kind of animal?"

"No, sir, it could not."

"Why? How long, or how much, is a cubit?"

He didn't know! He didn't know whether the cubit was ten feet or ten yards or ten inches. We closed the argument by saying with all the kindness we could muster, "If a child ten years of age manifested no more logic than you have shown in this argument, you would think he was wanting in intelligence. You have an ark *the size of which you do not know*. You have a number of animals, *which number cannot at this time be determined*. Yet you maintain that it is scientifically impossible to get two of an unknown number of creatures into a boat of undetermined capacity!"

The argument would have sounded silly to any listener who did not know the background, but it was sufficiently clear to his mind to start a train of logical thinking. We pointed out to him the depth of intelligence required to make a man reject the Bible on such flimsy grounds as he possessed. Like most men who start to reason, when his eyes were opened to the silliness of his position, he retracted his former statements upon making a study of the details that are given in the record.

Many times we have witnessed the attempt of ignorance to assail the Word of God, and it is always easily frustrated. The purpose of this treatise, however, is to deal seriously with objections to the story of the ark as they have been given to us so often by students and others, and to try to clear up several points.

The first consideration in our study here is the question of the capacity of the ark. The exact size of this famous vessel will probably never be known. Scholarship, knowledge, and the science of archeology have all contributed their quota of information, but we still do not know very much about the exact capacity of this marvelous craft. The text simply says: "And this is how thou shalt make it: the length of the ark three hundred cubits, the breadth of it fifty cubits, and the height of it thirty cubits." At first sight that seems enough and sufficiently specific, but now we face the question, "How long, or how much, is a cubit?"

Up to the present, this is a question that no scholar has been able to answer, although there are a number of opinions. The basis of measurement among the early Hebrews was a simple anatomical system. It seemed natural to base earliest measurements upon the parts of the body, and it is generally supposed that the "cubit" was the length of a man's forearm from the inside of the elbow to the tip of the longest finger. This, of course, would differ in various individuals, and confusion would result. This condition forced the adoption of a definite standard by the Jews and neighboring races, and in their later history Israel had a standardized cubit. Noah's ark, however, was built many years before the Jewish race began, and the standards of later years do not help us very much here.

There is also another possibility that we cannot ignore. The Scripture speaks of "the cubit of a man." Does Moses mean that the cubit Noah used was the length of a man, or was it the length of a forearm? The standard is variable, and it may have been either one. If the length of the ark was three hundred times the length of a man's forearm, we have one problem based on a certain set of factors. If the cubit that is here intended is the entire height of a man, however, we have still another problem with totally different and varying factors. If it was a man's height, how tall was the man?

It is a dangerous proceeding to make an argument from ignorance. How utterly senseless for the critics to say, "We do not know and cannot know the exact size of the ark, but we *do* know that it could not hold two of every kind of animal then living!"

The ark was a ship of gigantic size. To be conservative, we will take as a potential cubit the measurement advocated by the famous scientist and archeologist, William Mathew Petrie. He, being one of the foremost Egyptologists who ever lived, is entitled to speak with some authority, and he says the oldest standard cubit is twenty-two and a half inches. According to this basis, the ark was a tremendous and commodious boat. Five hundred and sixty-two feet and six inches long; ninety-three feet and six inches wide, fifty-six feet and three inches high. Built with a flat bottom, square on both ends and straight up the sides, there was no waste space in bow or stern, and it had the tremendous carrying capacity of a little over two million, nine hundred fifty-eight thousand cubit feet! (2,958,000 cubic feet). This is a tremendous cargo capacity. To put it in modern terms, it would take a train of almost 1,000 freight cars to carry this enormous load, or to provide this amount of cubic space!

That these dimensions and this size are not out of reason, we see from two separate lines of evidence. First, the ancient legendary stories of the ark make it much larger than this. It is inevitable that archeology should uncover traditional accounts of the deluge and the ark from the monuments and tablets of lost civilizations, for these ancient civilizations were founded, of course, by descendants of Noah. When people have a common origin, it is always shown in their common traditions, and as Noah and his sons were the only men saved alive from or through the flood, they must have peopled the entire earth with their progeny.

Indeed, there could have been no other way. That these common legends all point to a common origin, none can gainsay. Some of them are weird and distorted by tradition, but they all testify to two truths: *there was a deluge* and *there was an ark.*

The many Babylonian accounts of the ark differ in detail. One account, found on ancient clay tablets, described the ark as six stories high, with a mast on top. It had a rudder to steer with, and the whole was crowned by a superstructure, or dwelling. In addition to the presence of the builder and his wife, there was also a pilot who sailed with them. The structure was perfectly cubical, being 140 cubits each way. It was constructed in six stories, each having nine compartments. The clay tablets containing this account of the ark were dug up by George Smith in 1870, and were dated from the year 3,000 B. C. They are undoubtedly genuine.

The Greek historian Berosus also gives an exaggerated account of the ark. He describes it as three thousand feet long, and twelve thousand feet wide. He does not give its height.

The most fantastic account of the ark is the description of Origen, who had an extended controversy with a contemporary, whom he tried to silence by claiming that the ark was twenty-five miles long and three-quarters of a mile wide!

Many other tales and accounts could be introduced if we had unlimited time and space, but these must suffice to show the universal belief in the ark and its gigantic size. How simple and worthy of credence the language of the Bible seems to the reasoning modern mind, as we wade through all this ancient tradition dealing with the same subjects and facts! How our faith in the Book grows as we see the difference between an account which is dictated by God and a story man writes to suit his own fancy!

The ark was the largest vessel that ever floated prior to the building of the giant liners of the nineteenth and twentieth centuries. Because of its square construction, it could carry a third more cargo than any modern vessel that equalled it in size and dimensions. And when modern engine rooms, crew's quarters, control stations, life boats and safety belts, cabins, gymnasia, knife-edged bows and rounded sterns are all deducted, an ark of the size set forth (562 feet by 93 feet by 56 feet) would carry a much larger load than any ship of these approximate dimensions sailing the seas today.

The second factor in the problem is found in the size of the load. This factor is as variable as is the factor of capacity. The exact number of animals which were carried in the ark can never be determined by science. There may have been more "kinds" living then; certainly there could not have been less than are extant now. Birds, cattle, creeping things, are the only orders mentioned. The others are all grouped under the head of "every living thing of all flesh." Of the animals classified as "clean", there were to be fourteen, seven male and seven female. Of the other, or "unclean" animals, there were to be one pair, a male and a female of each.

Noah was not under the necessity of finding room in his ark for every *variety* and *specimen* of animal and bird alive today. As soon as we see this, the problem of the ark is simplified tremendously. The specific command is "*of each kind.*"

A kind is a species, and may be generally described as those which can cross-breed with fertility. Between any two "kinds" there is a line of demarcation closely drawn, and none may cross that line. The living things which can cross-breed or hybridize with fertility, are all related to that genus or "kind", and undoubtedly arose from the same parent ancestral stalk. The myriad *varieties* of each "kind" we see about us today have come by the process of mutation.

"What!" you say, "is not this evolution?" No, this is not evolution. Evolution is transmutation; and as long as the mutant, or variant, or variety under discussion does not cross that line of demarcation and become some other kind, it is just development and growth. There is a tendency to variation within the boundary of every species. The law of Mendel is based upon observations of this process of variation.

As a very common example of this process, we might cite the dahlia. The dahlia reproduces from a root-clump, which is erroneously called a bulb. This root-clump of the dahlia reproduces true to its type. For instance, if you have red dahlias in your garden this year and you save the root-clumps to plant the following season, from the root-clumps of the red dahlia you will get red dahlias of that type and variety. But the dahlia also produces seeds. When you plant the seeds from a red dahlia, you may get a dozen different colors of dahlia, none of which will be red. Of these mutants or variants, about two per cent will fix themselves as a new type and develop a root-clump that is established. Thus new varieties of dahlia are added to the market from year to year. You will note, however, that these new dahlias remain dahlias. They do not become onions or potatoes or tomatoes! As long as the dahlia produces new varieties of dahlia and not something else, we are dealing with mutation. When the dahlia, by an infinite number of changes, produces something which is *not* a dahlia, we will then have a case of transmutation. So far as the records of science go, this process of transmutation has never occurred.

Now then, if Noah took into his ark a pair of a pure strain of every available creature, the varieties would have arisen by the process of mutation. A typical case in point may be the bee. There are many, many different varieties of bees. But Noah would have to take only a fertile queen into the ark, for her progeny could in turn give rise to all the other varieties. This statement has been objected to on the ground that the queen bee does not care for or raise her own brood, but this work is done by the "workers" of the hive. This is unquestionably the present condition; *but how did the first pair of bees raise their young?*

If we admit that the bees were created like all other creatures, there was a male and a queen, and from them came all the bees. If you insist that the bees evolved out of some other lower insect, then the problem remains the same; there was a first *true bee*, and it had to perpetuate its kind.

There is a species of ant known as the Atta, of whom Beebe has written so engagingly in his book, "The Edge of the Jungle." These ants have a queen, who lays the eggs from which the workers hatch and rear the young. But when starting a new colony, the queen begins all by herself, laying the eggs and rearing the young unaided, until she has enough workers reared to take over the task, after which she degenerates to a mere egg-laying machine. It is evident that the first bees must have had some such method of procedure as this.

Another case may be the dogs. If Noah took the original strain into the ark, a male and a female, they would give rise to the other varieties of dogs. From one pair of canines, the process of mutation would soon produce all the many different breeds of dog so familiar now, and it is not too much to say that the present varieties of man and each other kind of living creatures could have arisen, and undoubtedly did arise, from an original pair of each kind. So in the case of Noah, he need not crowd his ark with a pair of every known variety, but just take two of the pure strain of each species.

True species are few. Varieties are many. But even of the true species there are some which would not have had to enter the ark. We can see no reason why the ducks could not survive out in the rain, unless certain geological cataclysms that probably attended the deluge would make it impossible. Certainly the rain would not drive them in. The alligators and crocodiles can live in salt water or fresh, or they prefer a mixture of both. They prefer their diet well ripened, so they would fare well outside the ark. The fish would be safe outside, and the barnacles could find a home on the bottom of the ark! In other words, a little analysis of the text shows that Ignorance loses its battle against Revelation here, for as always, Reason is the champion of the latter.

If half of the ark had been filled with food, and fourteen individuals of every true species now inhabiting that part of the world were stored in the other half of the ark, there would have been an average of 175 cubic feet of space for every individual! This would have been more than ample, as a 200 pound man requires only 15 cubic feet.

The problem is further simplified when we consider that Noah may not have had to provide space for animals not indigenous or native to the "world" he and the rest of the human race occupied. In the next chapter we will set forth the evidence that seems to show that the flood, coming as a judgment upon man for his sin, may have been limited to the world that was occupied by man. Since the dispersion did not take place until a long time after the flood, the civilization that perished was probably a local one. But as the only men alive were restricted to that locality, in the sense here intended, their habitation was "the world." So Noah would have to provide room in the ark for only those animals which lived there in the flooded locality. Who can say how many true species there were? The only comprehensive natural history survey of the land in which Noah lived was made by Dr. Howard Osgood. He found that there were just 575 varieties of mammals and birds between the size of a mouse and the size of a sheep, and 290 varieties between the size of a sheep and the size of a camel. There are no animals larger than a camel extant in that land today.

Food they had in plenty. It is evident that they would have no meat diet, as in Genesis the diet of all is given as the same: a vegetarian fare exclusively. See Genesis 1:29, 30 — "And God said, Behold, I have given you every herb yielding seed, which is upon the face of all the earth, and every tree, in the which is the fruit of a tree yielding seed; to you it shall be for food: and to every beast of the earth and to every bird of the heavens, and to everything that creepeth upon the earth, wherein there is life, I have given him every green herb for food; and it was so."

After the flood this law was changed and flesh was eaten, but up to the time of the flood this law was not violated, as far as we can find out. In another publication*, we have seen that

*See "The Canopied Earth", by Kellogg

there was a physical and scientific reason for the change to meat, but Noah's problem in provisioning the ark was a simple one. That he had plenty of food we can readily see, when we remember that he had had a hundred and twenty years in which to make hay!

A very wise and learned lady once said to us, "Tell your readers how the ark was ventilated! I have always worried about that! There were all those animals and men, and only one little window way up in the roof. How did they breathe?" Skepticism has often used this apparent weakness in the structure of the ark as an opportunity to point the finger of derision and raise the cry of improbability whenever the ark was mentioned. In a recent debate with Dr. Cantrell on the "Scientific Infallibility of Genesis", he ignorantly stated, "The ark was hermetically sealed!" The Scripture does not so state. Note the language of the text, and you will see two lines of thought worthy of deep analysis. Of course, the exact method of ventilation is not given in detail. This is a record of tremendous events and, as such, does not deal with small details. Histories of great battles do not bother themselves with the fit of the soldiers' clothes, whether their shoes fastened with laces or buttons, and such variety of minor details. Only the main facts are given, as in this present account.

We have the dimensions of the ark, and the shape. A word about these later on. Let us now look at the simple details of the actual construction. It contains this direction: "A window shalt thou make in the ark, and to a cubit shalt thou finish it upward." (Or, "Up to a cubit shalt thou finish it.")

Finish what?

The window of the ark?

If the window is to be finished up to a cubit, that probably means it ran the length of the ark to within a cubit of the end. That would be quite some ventilation! But if the words "finish it" refer to the ark itself, we have somewhat the same result. If the walls of the ark are finished "up to a cubit", that will leave an open ventilator all the way around the ark, twenty-two and a half inches wide! In either case, we have an open ventilator providing 2,460 square feet of air space, which is certainly ample. The overhanging eaves would keep the dripping rain out. There is no wind mentioned until the rain stopped, so no rain would drive in. That would be more than sufficient for comfort, and plenty for sanitation. Do not think that the modern sanitary engineer could add to the structure of the ark, for while the builder was Noah, the Architect and Designer was God.

The scientific accuracy of the ark is finally attested by its modern dimensions. The ancients did not so build ships. The ark was exactly six times as long as it was wide. Upon these identical proportions do we build our naval vessels today. In the days when we were in personal daily contact with the Pacific Fleet, the matchless pride of the American Navy was the U. S. S. New Mexico. Many, many times we have been on her decks, in her wardroom and gun turrets, and she was then the peer of anything afloat. She was built upon the scientific dimensions of Noah's ark!

Look up to the floating palaces that swim the waters today, and see how nearly they conform to this pattern. Six times as long as they are wide.

The ancients did not follow this plan. Their rule seemed to be their fancy! The ancient Phoenicians were the parents of navigation and shipcraft, and according to scanty records, they built a boat about twice as long as its width.

When Rome entered the First Punic Wars, she had a fleet of three hundred and thirty vessels — biremes, triremes, and quadriremes. These were built after a plan which varied from a length of a hundred and ten feet with a width of eleven feet, to a maximum of one hundred thirty feet long by twelve feet wide, or a general plan of ten times the width for the length. None of the ancients seem to have constructed on the proportions of the ark. Modern science figured them out for the U. S. S. New Mexico, and God revealed them all to Noah.

Modern Science and the Deluge

CHAPTER VII

Modern Science and the Deluge

NO MODERN railroad would consider itself in operating condition without a full and efficient system of mechanical signals. As you speed along the right of way on any modern railroad at night, the brilliant lights flash like scintillating jewels in rapid sweeps of color, telling the story of safety or danger. Green for promises of peace, and red for death and danger; the signals are there to be observed and obeyed! We believe the Omnipotent Godhead has a signal system in this world in which we live. Credit Him with at least as much intelligence as a railroad superintendent, and you must see that He does not expect His people to rush headlong through the night which leads to eternal day, without signals by the right of way.

A physical voice is the only one to which man gives heed. It may very well be that when there is a threatened collapse in the moral world, God sends physical disaster as a warning sign. Since man will not heed a spiritual plea, but is very tender in the care of his flesh, it is sometimes necessary to send disaster to call man back to the path of duty. In the providence of God there are three signals that we do well to heed

The first is earthquake. No human power can control or bring about earthquakes. We have often been in cities that were shaken by temblors, and have seen the wreck of some of the finest dwelling places and business buildings the ingenuity of man can devise. In a few seconds, while the hearts of sleepy folks stood still with terror, while no human hand could possibly aid them, the great concrete structures crashed and shattered to ruins in the street below. Men and women grabbed their babies and fled blindly for shelter — they knew not where. No human power can stay an earthquake, or even warn of its coming. It is a red light from God flashing in urgent warning. We believe it a solemn admonition from the Deity Who rules this world, and when moral collapse threatens, this physical warning is given.

Famine is another spectre that stalks the footsteps of man, which no human power can control. Diversified farming, rotation of crops, animal husbandry, scientific distribution of harvests; all must fail without the providence of God. A man may plant — the result is largely out of his hands. If God withholds the rain, the seeds will not grow. If He sends too much rain, the seeds will not grow. There is no clearer evidence of man's dependence upon his Maker than this: we feed from His hand.

If all the crops of all the world were gathered into one central storehouse and the whole human race were put upon starvation rations—

just enough to keep them alive — every edible thing would be consumed within eighteen months. If in that time God withheld the rain and obscured the sun or flooded all the fields, life would perish from the face of the earth. We talk about men being "far away from God!" The whole world must stay close to Him, and the farthest we can get away is a year and a half!

These things being so, and it must be conceded that they are indisputable facts, our generation has seen as great a folly as ever was committed by supposedly intelligent men. Disregarding every warning of history, ignoring every tragedy of past generations, and gambling not only the destiny, the prosperity, and welfare, but the very life of a whole people, certain blind leaders have wilfully destroyed the very necessities of life. In the godless philosophy of economy that is called "planned economy", men have ruthlessly slaughtered food animals, plowed under the growing grain, and hired the blinded yeomanry to allow their fields to lie idle. We cannot help remembering that once seven years of plenty, in the mightiest land then existing, were followed by seven years of want. God has nowhere promised that He would never again send famine upon any nation. If the heavens should once more turn to brass and the rains refuse to fall, so that the spectre of hunger stalked throughout our once prosperous land, we would have no just cause of complaint against Divine Providence, Who has desired, apparently, to send us more than we can use. It may be well to remember this, in case tragedy and dearth come upon us in place of the prosperity so foolishly promised.

Famine is a danger signal from God. When moral collapse threatens in the spiritual world, this red light of death and danger sometimes flashes to bring men back to a sense of obligation to God.

Flood is the third major tragedy that man cannot entirely control. No later than the year 1936, America stood appalled with the sudden sweep of mighty waters that rushed through the states of Pennsylvania, Ohio, Arkansas, and other portions of our vast country. Sweeping with that dull moan that creates terror in the most stalwart breast, swirling brown waters with irresistible force destroyed some of the most beautiful edifices that had been constructed by human hands, and still a complacent government talks about "flood control."

Like earthquakes and famine, a flood comes from circumstances beyond the control of man. Dams may be built to hold back the waters, but dams break; and the most disastrous flood we ever saw occurred when a dam that men called perfect broke with the sudden strain of waters from a cloudburst. Many lives were lost, homes were destroyed, ranches literally swept away, and live stock drowned. Floods are warnings from God. It may well be that when danger threatens in the moral world God Himself flashes these red lights of warning in the physical world, because the physical voice is the only voice that men will hear!

The Bible repeatedly states that earthquakes, famine, and floods are acts of God, and the in surance companies of the twentieth century recognize them as such! Sometimes they are punitive and sometimes admonitory, but they are beyond the control of man. The deluge of Noah is a case in point. This was the most disastrous catastrophe that ever struck the world in which we live, and it came because "God looked and saw that every imagination of the heart of man was evil in His sight continually!" The antediluvian world civilization was wiped out, because it refused to hear the voice of God. God spoke His warning to them through the prophet Noah for a hundred and twenty years, but the sin and self-confidence of the people were so deeply rooted that they laughed at both God and the prophet. The result was death and destruction.

But some will say: "The flood of Noah's time was merely traditional, and you can't build a case on tradition." Indeed, we had a young student in a midwestern college tell us that the entire book of Genesis was pure tradition and Hebrew folk-lore, and there never was a flood! (It took him four years of study to learn that; it took forty minutes so to tangle him up in the fallacy of his foolish arguments that he abandoned the four years' position!). We have had other wise folk tell us the same thing in many places, but they could never prove their case. The flood of the day of Noah is not tradition; it is fact. It stands today scientifically attested!

There is a law covering the presentation of evidence in civil courts that is extremely applicable to this argument. This law is expressed in these words: "Documents purporting to come from high antiquity and bearing upon their face no evident marks of forgery, if found in the proper repository, are deemed by the law to be authentic and credible, and the burden of proof to the contrary devolves upon the objector."

The documents containing the record of the flood are part of the Old Testament. Their history can be traced back in an unbroken chain of records to the fifteenth century before Christ. These documents bear upon their face the strongest evidence of authenticity and credibility, and have been received by every generation in turn as not only reliable but infallible. Some of the shrewdest intellects at the command of infidelity have again and again sought to assail the historic value of these documents without success.

The proper repository for religious records, in the sense intended by the law, would be in the church. The proper repository for military records would be in the department of the army, just as the proper repository for naval records would be the archives of the secretary of the navy. In the legal sense, the proper repository for records of real estate transactions would be the county courthouse. In exactly that sense, the church is legally recognized as the proper repository for ancient documents dealing with the things of religion. So unless some new evidence is discovered which will unqualifiedly prove beyond any legal doubt that the writings of the Old Testament are forgeries, they have a legal right to stand in a court of law and be received at their face value. However, so sure are the proponents of Genesis that the records are credible, that they are willing and ready always to accept the burden of proof and dispute with the objector by the presentation of evidence that cannot be gainsaid. The historicity of the flood account in the book of Genesis can be established beyond question by evidence from three recognized branches of modern science. The mass and detail of this evidence is so overwhelming that books can be written, and have been written, upon this subject. So in the space of this short chapter we will only summarize the evidence of these three sciences.

The first of the sciences which establish the credibility of the record of the deluge is the science of ethnology. This is the science which deals with living races, with their customs and racial origins, and with the peculiarities that distinguish one race from another. Ethnologists are agreed upon two basic principles. One is that when widely isolated peoples have in common a body of tradition and belief, that common possession establishes relationship or common ancestry. The other conclusion is that when widely separated peoples all have a common tradition or belief in a certain past event, that common consent of tradition establishes the fact that there was some historical occurrence as the basis of this belief.

No ethnologist would gainsay the fact that every living race which has been made a subject of study does have an account of the flood that occurred in the day of Noah. If the Biblical account is true, this fact can easily be accounted for, as all living races came by lineal descent from the sons of Noah who were saved with him in the ark, and they handed the same story down to their descendants in all its essential details. Some of these races have progressed and developed since the sons of Noah gave them birth, and others have degenerated; but they all retain their accounts of the flood.

For the student who is interested in this subject, there are no less than thirty-three separate racial records that may be consulted among people and races who are living today. Of this large number of independent witnesses, only two, the Egyptian and the Scandinavian records, fail to coincide absolutely with the Biblical account of destruction by water. The Scandinavian and the Egyptian records give a partial destruction by water and the balance by the direct action of the gods. In this same list of records, carefully reviewed, only five of these present nations have some other traditional method of the rescue of the remnant than by the ark, with some original details. Of this number, one of these nations makes no record of the salvation of the human seed, while three others conform but partially to the Scriptural account. Three of these records fail to mention the preservation of animal life, while one other has only a partial correspondence to the record as given in Genesis. Again, in this long list of independent evidences, the ark, in all except three cases, landed on a mountain. Only four of these records contain no statement as to the birds being sent out to bring back to the survivors the welcome news of the recession of the flood. Three of these records, again, say nothing of the divine favor which dwelt upon the survivors, while only two of them fail to record the worship of the saved remnant when they came forth from the ark.

It is manifestly impossible, in the brevity of this chapter, to give the complete details of all of these many ethnological testimonies; so we will content ourselves with just a few.

The Polynesian record closely parallels the Biblical account. While we were in the Islands some time ago, we became intensely interested in the folk-lore and traditions of the natives, and we were most fortunate in acquiring the "Fornander Collection of Hawaiian Antiquities and Folk-Lore," published by the Bishop Museum. In Volume Six, Number Two, Third Series, Part Two, there is given the ancient Polynesian account of the flood.

The hero of the account is one Nuu (pronounced noo-oo, a close approach to No-ah). In obedience to the commands of the god Kane, Nuu built a large vessel with a house on it, and it was called "Waa Hulau." In this craft, accompanied by his wife Lili-Noe, he rode out the deluge in safety. When the flood subsided, the three gods, Kane, Ku, and Lono, entered this "ark" and told Nuu to get out. He did so, and found himself on top of Mount Mauna Kea on the island of Hawaii. He dwelt in a cave there, and called the cave after his wife, Lili-Noe, and the cave remains as proof, to this very day!

When Nuu left the ark, he took with him a pig, coconuts, and *awa* as an offering to his god, Kane. (Note that the ark must have contained animals, and he follows the action of Noah in sacrifice.) As he left the ark, he looked up and saw the moon, and thought that it was the face of Kane; so he offered his pig, coconuts, and *awa* to the moon. Kane was very angry, and came down to punish him. The path he came down was a rainbow, and when Nuu explained his mistake, Kane went back to heaven over his rainbow path, but he left the rainbow as a sign of forgiveness. This is a close parallel to the Genesis account. Nuu had three sons (another parallel) and as all the rest of mankind died in the flood, he became the progenitor of a new race.

The American Indians are very evidently of Mongolian or Asiatic origin, and they have traditions of the flood and its destruction of all life except a remnant; which Indian tradition bears a close resemblance to the Chinese. The one Indian legend with which we are best acquainted is the Modoc record. Their story is of a man who floated his family on a raft of logs, while he picked up swimming animals of different kinds until he had two of each. He landed after many days of adventure on a high mountain, and from him and his rescued remnant the world was repopulated. We have heard other legends, however, from those who have worked with other tribes, and with some minor changes the story is essentially the same.

The Chinese account is found in the book of Li-Ki. It has many similarities with the Genesis account, ascribing as the cause of the flood the wickedness of man, who despised the councils and laws of heaven. It gives the same causes for the flood from nature, saying the flood came when "the pillars of heaven were broken . . . the earth fell to pieces, and the waters enclosed within its bosom burst forth with violence, and overflowed." A goodly remnant were saved, and re-peopled the earth.

The Descent of Manu embodies the account of the flood in India. The warning was given to Manu by a great fish who said, "A deluge will sweep all creatures away. Build a vessel and worship me, and when the waters arise, enter the vessel and I will save you." This Manu did, and when the flood began, the fish towed the vessel to the mountains of the North, where they fastened it to a tree, and as the waters descended they floated down. Since all save Manu died in the flood, he peopled the earth anew.

From British East Africa a friend writes us a weird account of a legend concerning the flood. From the wilds of the South American jungles, we are given a tribal tradition of the deluge. In the early records of Spanish explorers, in the Islands of the sea and the mainlands of new continents, we read of traditions of the flood, and even from the primitive Malays the record is the same. The summary is plain:

Whenever we find a similarity of account from living witnesses, we say the story is true and the fact proved. All living races tell us there was a deluge; the witnesses agree; the fact stands established.

The second science which clamors to be heard on this matter is the science of archeology, which bears the same striking testimony. As ethnology is the science of the records and customs of living races, so archeology is the science of races that are dead and gone. The men who have lived and labored, and who left their works covered by the dust of ages, still speak with a clarion voice from the tongueless records of forgotten things. Many wondrous testimonies to the inspiration of the Bible have been advanced by this science, for every time we sink a spade into an ancient dwelling of a past age, we find new light on the customs and histories of other days. In Egypt, in ancient

Britain, in Palestine, in Asia and Asia Minor, in South America and North America, the archeologists have been gathering startling confirmation of the truth of the Genesis account of creation and its record of men.

The first voice we offer now is that of ancient Babylonia. We give this witness first because it is the most striking and complete. This record is dated from about 3000 B.C. We have previously mentioned the clay tablets discovered by George Smith in 1870. These cuneiform tablets told the story of the flood in hundreds and hundreds of words. It was an unabridged account, the heart of which we give here. The blank spaces represent words that could not be made out in the broken segments of the tablets.

"(Izdubar) to him also speaks even to Xisuthrus afar off: O Xisuthrus, (why) dost thou not again (to me) as I (to thee)? (why) dost thou not again (to me) as I (to thee)? * * * my heart to make war * * * I come up after thee, when thou didst take, and in the assembly of the gods didst obtain life.

"Xisuthrus to him also speaks, even to Izdubar: Let me reveal to thee (Izdubar) the story of my preservation, and the judgment of the gods let me relate to thee. The city Surippak the city which thou knowest on the Euphrates is placed, that city is ancient and the gods are within it. To make a deluge (*or* whirlwind) the great gods have brought their heart; even he their father, Anu, their king, the warrior Bel, their throne-bearer, Ninip, their minister, the lord of Hades, Nin-si-kha (wife of) Hea with them sat, and their will he (*i.e.* Hea) repeated: to his minister the minister of the city of Kis, he declared what he had (in mind); his minister heard and proclaimed attentively: Man of Surippak, son of Ubara-tutu, build a house, make a ship to preserve the sleep of plants (and) living beings; store the seed and vivify life, cause also the seed of life of every kind to go up into the midst of the ship. The ship which thou shalt make, 600 cubits (shall be) its measure in length, 60 cubits the amount of its breadth and its height * * * and on the deep cover it, even it, with a roof. I understood and say to Hea my lord: the building of the ship which thou commandest thus, * * * I shall have made, * * * the sons of the host and the old men. (Hea opened his mouth and) speaks and says to me his servant: * * * thou shalt say unto them, * * * he has rejected me and * * * it is upon me * * * like caves * * * may I judge above and below * * * close the ship * * * at the season which I will make known to you, into it enter and the door of the ship turn. Into the midst of it thy grain, thy furniture, thy goods, thy wealth, thy woman slaves, thy handmaids, and the sons of the host, (the beasts) of the field, the wild animals of the field, as many as I would protect, I will send to thee, and thy door shall guard (them).

"Adrakhasis his mouth opened and speaks, and says to Hea his lord: No one a ship has made. * * * in the lower part of the ship has shut up * * * and may I see the ship * * * in the lower part of the ship * * * the building of the ship which thou commandest me (thus), which in * * *

"strong * * * on the fifth day * * * it rose. In its circuit 14 in all (were) its girders. 14 in all it contained * * * above it I placed its roof, it * * * I enclosed it. I rode in it the sixth time; I divided its passages the seventh time; its interior I divided the eighth time. Leaks for the waters within it I cut off. I saw the rents and the wanting parts I added. 3 *sari* of bitumen I poured over the outside. 3 *sari* of bitumen I poured over the inside. 3 *sari* of men carrying baskets, who carried on their heads food. I added a *saros* of food which the people should eat; two *sari* of food the boatmen shared. To * * * I sacrificed oxen I (established) * * * each day I (established) * * * beer, food, and wine; (I collected them) like the waters of a river, and (I collected) like the dust of the earth, and (in the ship) the food with my hand I placed. (Through the help of) Samas the seaworthiness of the ship was accomplished. * * * they were strong and the tackling of the ship I caused to bring above and below. * * * they went in two-thirds of it.

"All I possessed I collected it, all I possessed I collected it in silver, all I possessed I collected it in gold, all I possessed I collected it in the seed of life of all kinds. I caused everything to go up into the ship, my slaves and my handmaids, the beast of the field, the wild animal of the field, the sons of the people all of them, I caused to go up. The season Samas fixed and he spake saying: In the night I will cause it to rain from heaven heavily, enter into the midst of the ship and shut thy door. That season came round, (of which) he spake saying: In the night I will cause it to rain from heaven heavily. Of the day I reached its evening, the day of watching fear I had. I entered into the midst of the ship and shut my door. On closing the ship to Buzur-sadi-rabi the boatman the habitation I gave with its goods.

"Mu-seri-ina-namari arose, from the horizon of heaven a black cloud. Rimmon in the midst of it thundered, and Nebo and the Wind-god went in front, the throne-bearers went over the mountain and plain, Nergal the mighty removes the wicked, Ninip goes in front, he casts down, the spirits of earth carried destruction, in their terror they shake the earth; of Rimmon his flood reached to heaven. The darkened (earth to a waste) was turned,

"the surface of the earth like * * * they covered, (it destroyeth all) living beings from the face of the earth; the raging (deluge) over the people, reached to heaven. Brother saw not his brother, men did not know one another. In heaven the gods feared the whirlwind and sought a refuge; they ascended to the heaven of Anu. The gods like dogs were fixed, in a heap did they lie down. Spake Istar like a child, the great goddess uttered her speech: All to clay are turned and that which I in the presence of the gods prophesied (even evil has happened). As I prophesied in the presence of the gods evil, to evil (were devoted) all my people, the trouble I prophesied thus: I the mother have begotten my people and like the young of the fishes they fill the sea. And the gods because of the spirits of earth are weeping with me. The gods on seats are seated in lamentation, covered were their lips for the coming evil. Six days and nights passed, the wind, the whirlwind, (and) the storm, overwhelmed. On the seventh day at its approach the rain was stayed, the raging whirlwind which had smitten like an earthquake, was quieted. The sea began to dry, and the wind and deluge ended. I watched the sea making a noise, and the whole of mankind was turned to clay, like reeds the corpses floated. I opened the window, and the light smote upon the fortress of my nostrils. I was grieved and sat down; I weep, over the fortress of my nostrils went my tears. I watched the regions at the boundary of the sea, towards all the twelve points of the compass (there was) no land. In the country of Nizir rested the ship; the mountain of Nizir stopped the ship, and to pass over it it was not able. The first day, the second day, the mountain of Nizir stopped the ship. The third day, the fourth day, the mountain of Nizir stopped the ship. The fifth day, the sixth day, the mountain of Nizir stopped the ship. On the seventh day at its approach

"I sent forth a dove and it left. The dove went, it returned, and a resting-place it did not find, and it came back. I sent forth a swallow and it left. The swallow went, it returned, and a resting-place it did not find, and it came back. I sent forth a raven and it left. The raven went, and the carrion on the water it saw, and it did eat, it swam, and turned away, it did not come back. I sent (the animals) forth to the four winds, I sacrificed a sacrifice, I built an altar on the peak of the mountain, by sevens vessels I placed, at the bottom of them I spread reeds, pines, and juniper. The gods smelt the savour, the gods smelt the good savour; the gods like flies over the sacrificer gathered. From afar also the great goddess at her approach lifted up the mighty arches (*i.e.* the rainbow) which Anu had created as his glory. The crystal of those gods before me (*i.e.* the rainbow) never may I forget;

"those days I devised with longing that I might never forget. 'May the gods come to my altar, may Bel never come to my altar, for he did not consider and had made a whirlwind, and my people he consigned to the abyss.' From afar also Bel at his approach saw, the ship he stopped; Bel was filled with anger against the gods and the spirits of heaven: 'Let no one come out alive, never may a man live in the abyss.' Ninip his mouth opened, and spake; he says to the warrior Bel: 'Who is it except Hea that forms a resolution? and Hea knows and all things he * * *' Hea his mouth opened and spake, he says to the warrior Bel: 'Thou messenger of the gods, warrior, as thou didst not consider a deluge thou madest. The doer of sin bore his sin, the blasphemer bore his blasphemy. Never may the just prince be cut off, never may the faithful (be destroyed). Instead of thy making a deluge, may lions come and men be diminished; instead of thy making a deluge, may hyaenas come and men be diminished; instead of thy making a deluge, may a famine happen and the country be (destroyed); instead of thy making a deluge, may pestilence come and men be destroyed. I did not reveal the judgment of the gods. To Adrahasis (Xisuthrus) a dream I sent, and the judgment of the gods he heard.' Again also Bel considers, (*literally,* again consideration was considered); he approaches the midst of the ship. He took my hand and caused me to ascend up, he caused (me) to ascend; he united my wife to my side; he turned unto us and fixes himself in covenant with us; he approaches us: 'Formerly Adrakhasis (was) mortal, but again also Adrakhasis and his wife to live as gods are taken away, and Adrakhasis also dwells in a remote place at the mouth of the rivers.' They took me, and in a remote place at the mouth of the rivers they caused me to dwell."

There are many of these Babylonian traditions which differ strikingly in their details. We might mention a second Babylonian flood record, the hero of which was one Gilgamesh, who lived in a city noted for sin and violence. Warned by Ishtar of an approaching deluge, he followed instructions and tore down his house to build an ark. In it he took "seed of every kind of life." His ark was cubic, 140 cubits each way, and had a mast and pilot-house. He finished the ark and made it water-tight with pitch or bitumen. When the gods repented of their anger, they turned the ark into the mountains of Armenia (called in Genesis, "the mountains of Ararat"), where the man and his wife re-peopled the earth. The similarity to the Genesis account is striking.

Egyptian records also have been recovered. The ancient Egyptian account tells how a great flood wiped out all mankind except a few wandering shepherds who escaped under the protection of the gods by climbing to the high mountains of Armenia. This flood was sent by the god "Ra' the Creator", who was angered by the insolence of man. He repented of his deed, and swore never to destroy the race again.

The Druidic legends of ancient Britain tell of a flood which the Supreme Being sent on the earth because of the gross sin of mankind. The waves of the sea came higher than the hills of Britain, and the rain fell from the clouds in such violence that the waters soon covered the earth. One ancient patriarch, a man of high piety, was shut up in a stout ship with a select company of worshippers, and after riding safely through the cataclysm, these few peopled the earth with its present population.

The oldest written record of the flood is in the Sumerian legends, and as evidence of their accuracy we print this recent discovery.

Science Supports Flood Story in Bible

New York, March 16, 1936—(A.P)—The Biblical story of the flood has the support of material evidence unearthed by science.

Returning from an archeological expedition to Mesopotamia, Professor C. Leonard Woolley said he had found an eight-foot layer of silt and clay deposited during an overflowing of the Euphrates river and the Biblical deluge.

Professor Woolley headed an expedition of the Museum of the University of Pennsylvania and the British Museum, which with a crew of 160 Arab workmen has been engaged for seven years in excavating the ruins of ancient Sumeria.

Penetrating through a layer of evidence indicating a highly developed civilization of about 4000 B. C., they suddenly came upon a layer of silt or sand in which all manifestations of human life ceased to exist. Beneath this deposit were utensils in the native fashion and expertly molded brick, indicating a high peak of cultural development.

Professor Woolley emphasized that he attempted to prove nothing by his findings.

"We are not out to prove anything or disprove anything," he said. "If we were, we would be bad archeologists. We, scientists, use the things we dig up with any other kind of information which may be forthcoming. In this case the previous information was in Genesis and the Sumerian and Babylonian legends.

"The eight-foot deposit of clay in three places as much as 200 yards apart can only have resulted from a flood of unexampled magnitude, and this can only be the flood of Sumerian legend and history, the flood of the book of Genesis."

Professor Woolley said his discovery would indicate that the flood was not universal, but declared, "neither does the Bible story, properly understood, make any such claim."

Genesis Record:	**Archeological Records:**
There was a deluge.	There was a deluge.
The race of mankind was destroyed.	The race of mankind perished.
A remnant was saved.	A select few escaped.
These escaped by divine aid.	They escaped through the care of the gods.
A warning was given.	The remnant was warned.
An ark was built.	A boat was made.
Animal life was preserved.	Animals were saved with the man.
The ark floated under divine care.	The boat was saved by the gods.
The ark landed in the mountains of Ararat.	The boat landed in the Armenian mountains.
The released remnant sacrificed.	The saved few worshipped with sacrifice.
The flood came because of sin.	The deluge came because of human failure.
God promised not to destroy man again.	The gods repented and pledged peace.
A sign was given.	A sign was given.
The saved few re-people the earth	All men came from these few.

And finally, both agree that the causes of the flood were rain and marine catastrophe.

As in the case of ethnology, the witnesses all agree. When we find such parallel agreement in legends among ancient people, we decide they lived together or had a common ancestry. So in this marvelous harmony of Scripture and legend, we only not see proof of the reality and historicity of the deluge, but we have the additional proof of common ancestry for all Noah's descendants.

The third science whose testimony we would introduce is geology. The testimony of geology will be of great value, for geology is the science which deals with the physical earth. If there was a great cataclysmic deluge, the earth must bear some record of that fact, and never doubt but that the earth does! Those who laugh at the Genesis account of the flood, do so out of the depths of profound ignorance of geology. Many scores of students have asked us, "If the account of a flood in the Bible is history, why is there no record of it in geology?" The answer is that there is such a record.

There is the same harmony of opinion (?) among geologists that characterizes the other sciences; but most of them admit a world-catastrophe; which was probably the deluge. One authority claims that this was the cause of the glacial age, and builds a convincing and ingenious theory on the weight of water and its effect on the climate of the earth. Several others, equally authoritative, disagree, and say the flood came as a result of the collapse of the giant ring of ice that once encircled this globe like a tremendous lens. Others claim the deluge was only local, and the merry battle goes on. But whatever theory geologists may hold, they almost all agree that there was a flood.

The most up-to-date book of geology extant today is "The New Geology; a Textbook for Colleges," by G. McCready Price. If you haven't read this you are behind the times that much, and you ought to read it at once. This book is a masterpiece of real science, and explodes in a convincing manner some of the ancient fallacies of science "falsely so called." Dr. Price gives much space to the evidences from geology and proves conclusively that there was a flood. I will not here review his arguments; get the book and read it.

There were undoubtedly two causes for the flood. The first was precipitation. It rained for forty days and nights. The significance of this is seen when we remember that up to that time there had apparently been no rain upon the earth, but " a mist arose and watered the land." How utterly incomprehensible must Noah's warning have sounded to the antediluvians when he said, "Flee from the flood! The heavens will rain water!" They never saw rain, and had absolutely no conception of it. So men today will not heed the warning of Peter when he says, "The earth is reserved for the fire of judgment, that will destroy all flesh!"

It never had rained. According to Vail's theory, around the globe there was a protecting lens of ice that made the whole world an Eden of tropical splendor. It was a "firmament" indeed; and rain could not come through it. The rays of the sun that cause decay were strained out, and long life was the rule. These rays also cause fermentation, and Noah, who was accustomed to drinking the juice of the grape in the days before the flood, was amazed when the fermented juice made him drunk! In that wondrous atmosphere, life was so easily sustained that men ate no meat, but a vegetable diet was the rule. Then the catastrophe came. The great ring melted and descended in a torrent of water and ice. In some sections it fell as water, and a flood was the result. In other sections it collapsed as ice, and a condition of glaciation was the result. The whole matter is set forth in these simple words, pregnant with depths of meaning:

"And the windows of heaven were opened!"

For forty days and nights the waters fell, and this was one cause of the flood. It rained. We saw it rain twenty-two minutes once, and hundreds of thousands of dollars' damage resulted in the valleys below! Men said it was a cloudburst; in the days of Noah it rained thus for forty days and nights.

The second cause of the flood was geological. There have been many upheavals of the earth's surface and slippages of its crust; here was one of them. The level of the land sank, and the bottom of the sea was raised. This is implied in the statement, "The fountains of the great deep were broken up," and the waters prevailed on the face of the earth. The highest mountains were covered to a depth of fifteen cubits and death was the result.

It is evident at once that this upheaval, or slipping of the earth's crust, was the main cause of the flood. Noah began to build his ark in the valley near the mouth of the river, and when the waters had carried it to its final resting place, it was up in the Armenian mountains, in the Ararat range. It is thus evident the drift was from the sea to the land, and this current would nominally be caused by the influx of sea water.

The common laws of nature were here directed, as always, to serve the will of God. When the waters had prevailed a hundred and fifty days, God's thought turned again to Noah, and the flood was stopped. First, a wind swept out across the waters. Thus the rate of evaporation was greatly increased, and some waters lifted. Then the "windows of heaven were stopped," which provision kept the evaporated waters from precipitating again. And finally, the fountains of the deep were stopped. That can mean only one thing; the land level was shifted again, so that the sea went back to its former place, or nearly so.

Can this shifting of land levels be seen in the science of geology? Indeed it can. The unbelieving and materialistic scientist is hard pressed to understand this strange condition; there are mountains and cliffs that have been stood on their heads! The geologist claims that he knows the rock formations from the earliest to the latest, and classifies them *according to age*. The "oldest" rocks are on the bottom, of course, and the "youngest" rocks are on top. So we read the geological account like a calendar. This, of course, is an entirely gratuitous arrangement, and has caused a tremendous amount of confusion and trouble. What can any man know about the age of undated things he claims were made a hundred million years before there was a man to keep the record?

The confusion grows worse when we leave the textbooks and get out in field research, for then we see that the rocks with stubborn ignorance refuse to follow the chart laid down by the World Congress of Geology! In many places rocks one hundred million years old (?) are laid down on top of rocks only one million years old! And this according to the geologists' own way of reckoning. How did this happen? How could it happen? Why, the only possible way was for the earth's crust to slip and turn over. In some of our California formations, notably of the Eocene period, the strata of rock run straight up and down instead of across the mountain! When did this tremendous shift take place? Dr. Price says that it was at the time of the flood; and while we are not advancing that as a dogmatic statement, we can at least contend that the earth shows that there was not only one upheaval, such as Genesis sets forth, but two at least.

Was the deluge universal in extent? This is a question that has been asked by scores and hundreds of interested students. That seems to be the big theme in the minds of all who are confused, and are after some peg upon which to hang their faith. There is absolutely no evidence that will admit of an unqualified, dogmatic answer either way. At least, the deluge was as universal as the human race. If man was limited to the Euphrates valley, then the purpose of the flood would be accomplished in a deluge limited to that area. The object of the flood was judgment and death on the world of mankind, and the flood was as far reaching as human habitation. No man can say what that limitation was.

Philology does not help us much. A careful study of the Hebrew text does not give the basis for a positive answer. There are three Hebrew words of interest here. The first is *"erets"*.
This word appears in the Bible....2,282 times.
It is translated "land" ....1,356 times.
It is translated "earth" ....686 times.
It is translated "country".........140 times.
It is translated "ground" ....96 times.
It is translated "world" ....4 times.

The use of the words "country", "land", and "ground" are sometimes limited in extent and local in application, as "land of Palestine" or "country of the Jews". The words "earth" and "world" are usually universal in meaning.

This word appears in Genesis often. It is used of the world God created, thirty times. It is given to denote the extent of the flood, forty-six times. It may be either local or universal.

The word "*adamah*" next appears.

It occurs in the Bible..............223 times.
Translated "earth" ....53 times.
Translated "ground" ....43 times.
Translated "land" ....125 times.
Translated "farmer" ....1 time.
Translated "country" ....1 time.

This word is used nine times to denote the "world" the deluge destroyed. It may be either local or universal.

The word "*tebel*" appears in Hebrew Scripture thirty-six times. It is translated "world" thirty-five times, "habitation" once. It is almost always given as "the habitable world" and is never used in the Genesis account of the flood. An argument based on the absence of evidence or the lack of a word in the text is a shaky one; so we make none here. You must consider the facts and make your own conclusions. It is enough to know that the flood was as widespread as the race of man. They perished, because of sin and the judgment of God.

The city of Los Angeles was builded by Spanish pioneers in a semi-arid region surrounded by veritable deserts. When the city began its phenomenal modern progress, it became necessary to expend vast fortunes for the impounding of water to serve the needs of the populace.

One of the great dams which the city engineers constructed was in San Francisquito Canyon. The mouth of this canyon opened up into a fertile and charming valley, wherein were some of the loveliest homes and most prosperous farms in Southern California. The dam was a masterpiece of engineering skill and human ingenuity, but it had one unsuspected flaw. The bed rock to which the dam was anchored was a type of stone that is pervious to water. As the years rolled by, the water silently operated on the nature of this stone, until it softened it like putty.

One night in the deadest darkness, with no light but the stars to shine upon the scene of tragedy, the dam suddenly let go, all in one piece. With a roar like the trumpets of doom, a wall of water forty feet high went surging down the canyon from wall to wall on the unsuspecting and sleeping populace in the valley below. Fortunately, a watchman on the ridge heard the roar and saw the dam go out. He ran to a telephone and called the operator. With the assistance of the other courageous members of the telephone staff, she alarmed the sleeping farmers and the small hamlets that lay in the path of the oncoming flood.

The officers of the law went searching out through the darkness of the night with their sirens shrieking, to carry the warning to all those who had no telephones. The reader may know that in Southern California most of the itinerant labor consists of the Mexican population. These simple folk, whose wants are few and who are satisfied with almost as little as are the southern darkies, gather in temporary camps wherever there is work to be done. One little company of these humble folk had gathered in a depression in the valley to pitch their tents and to work upon the walnut crop. Into their midst in the dead of night the officers of the law came, with their alarming cry, "Flee to the hills; a flood is coming!"

It happened that most of these Mexicans were not familiar with the English language, and the spokesman, who might have been called the "jaffe politico", stepped forward to bear the message to his compatriots. He asked for a repetition of the statement, and the officer said "Flee to the hills; a flood is coming." Now this chap had a rare sense of humor and was noted for being somewhat witty. He prided himself upon his logic and his reason. He turned his face toward the bright, gleaming stars above, and with a quaint gesture held out his hand, palm upward. Then he laughed in the face of the deputies and said, "You big fool; she no rain!" And they all went back to bed. Forty minutes later, a wall of water, still twenty feet high, swept over the city where these happy and carefree unbelievers were sleeping the sleep of doom, and the rescue party found scarcely a body of those who were swept out to sea.

So it is in the day in which we now live. The Word of God solemnly warns men in these challenging words:

"Knowing this first, that there shall come in the last days scoffers, walking after their own lusts, and saying. Where is the promise of his coming? for since the fathers fell asleep, all things continue as they were from the beginning of the creation. For this they willingly are ignorant of, that by the word of God the heavens were of old, and the earth standing out of the water and in the water: Whereby the world that then was, being overflowed with water, perished: But the heavens and the earth, which are now, by the same word are kept in store, reserved unto fire against the day of judgment and perdition of ungodly men. But, beloved, be not ignorant of this one thing, that one day is with the Lord as a thousand years, and a thousand years as one day. The Lord is not slack concerning his promise, as some men count slackness; but is longsuffering to us-ward, not willing that any should perish, but that all should come to repentance."

Just as certainly as the ancient world perished in the flood, so this present age is reserved against that time when the fires of judgment shall smite and spare not. Yet when we today, who have the Gospel in our keeping, would warn men of their danger, they laugh us to scorn. We say to the lost, "Flee to the ark that is Jesus Christ, and escape the coming judgment." They in turn lift their faces to the blue sky of civilization, wherein twinkle the beaming lights of science and culture. They say, "You're a fool. Since the time of the fathers, all things have been as they now are." But alas! We know that while they sleep in this sleep of death, the judgment of God draweth nigh. We are persuaded of the reader of these words better things. May you heed the voice of the Spirit of God, and enter the ark of salvation by receiving Christ as your Saviour, before the next deluge of disaster comes, when the hand of God smites the sins of men.

Modern Science and the Long Day of Joshua

CHAPTER VIII

Modern Science and the Long Day of Joshua

ONE of the most difficult tasks that face the instructor is that of correcting a false impression which has become deeply rooted in the student mind. It is a lamentable fact that the present generation of college students has been so indoctrinated with the false idea that modern science and the Word of God are at hopeless variance, that it is a constant struggle to make the truth known to them. Some of the most childish ideas are offered as evidence and accepted by the credulous without investigation. Some of the most ignorant errors are joined with some of the most fallacious scientific fables, all to be presented as unquestionable proof, and are so received. The purpose of this mass of misinformation is to demonstrate that modern science has proved the Bible to be a book of folk-lore and myth.

We have always been ready and eager to answer all questions at any time, as far as our knowledge will permit. In student conferences we often meet the same questions over and over again, but there is no question that we have met oftener than the query concerning the long day of Joshua. This is perhaps the last and most frequently used argument which is directed against the authority, credibility, and scientific accuracy of the Bible. This record of the long day of Joshua has given rise to more argument and debate on the subject of inspiration than has any other single factor of the problem. Yet when Joshua's record is properly studied and all the evidence is weighed and considered, there is no chapter of the Book that is more valuable in establishing the truth and infallible character of the Scriptures, than is this one.

Many questions about this miracle occur, no doubt, because of the paucity of details in Joshua's account of the battle of Beth-horon. This ancient battle was one of the greatest that is recorded in the annals of history. The significance of this fact is largely overlooked, but there was no single battle in the recent world war that could compare with this one in far-reaching significance and results.

To some extent, every nation and land under the sun has been affected by Joshua's victory at Beth-horon. In this battle Joshua crushed the powerful league which opposed the people of Jehovah in their entrance into the land where Messiah must be born. As a result of Joshua's victory, the way was opened for prophecies to be fulfilled in the most literal fashion. The crushing victory of Joshua at Beth-horon was the means of the fulfillment of God's covenant with Abraham, and gave this land of Canaan to Israel. From this time on, the various battles of the Israelites might be referred to as "mopping up" operations, for this was the end of organized opposition.

The most powerful alliance of which the enemy were capable opposed Joshua on the plains of Beth-horon. When the five kings died there and the army of the allies was smashed, the entire land was open to the possession of the Children of Israel. As a result of that battle nations were exterminated. The citizenry, government, culture, and destiny of a great land were changed in that hour of victory.

Through the Hebrew conquest of the land of Canaan, even the destiny of the United States of America, then undreamed of, was definitely shaped. For as a result of this battle, Jesus was born (in accordance with the prophecies) in the land that then and there changed ownership.

This battle may be likened in its far-reaching effects to the Battle of Waterloo. Yet the entire account of Joshua's victory, from the setting forth of the army on their forced march from Gilgal until their return, is given in just two hundred and seventy-one words. There have been many more than that number of volumes written about the Battle of Waterloo! So the details in this account are necessarily meager. Every word in this record must be studied carefully, and the casual and careless reader will certainly think this account is highly improbable, without realizing that it is his own ignorance which makes it seem so.

The setting of the battle is of tremendous importance. The reader will recall that the book of Joshua contains the record of the conquest of the land of Canaan by the army of Israel. It would be of value at the outset of this study to refresh the memory with a summary of the account of this conquest, as given in the book of Joshua. Chapters one to five deal with the entrance of the people into the land, their preparation for the great conquest, and the consecration of the nation to this task. The story of the conquest really begins in chapter six, which deals with the capture of Jericho.

The strange incidents in connection with that event have long been a source of delight to the skeptic, who has imagined that the falling of the walls of Jericho constitutes a quaint fable and has no historical value. The light of the lamp of archeology, however, has illumined the events that transpired at Jericho and has established the record of the sixth chapter as being historically unquestionable. The great Marston expedition, under the leadership of Dr. Garstang, has not only established the historical accuracy of this sixth chapter of Joshua, but has brought to light details of the conquest that prove the book of Joshua to have been written by an eye-witness of the fall of Jericho. The ablest archeologists of the twentieth century have proved beyond question that the events of chapter six happened exactly as they were written by the pen of Joshua.

The seventh chapter deals with the defeat of Israel at Ai. The sin of Achan was then discovered and purged. As a result, in the eighth chapter the record is given of the capture of Ai and the extermination of its populace of some twelve thousand.

This recapitulation brings us to the stirring events of the ninth and tenth chapters of the book of Joshua. In the path of Joshua's march of conquest, there were six great and powerful nations. These nations are named as the Hittite, Amorite, Canaanite, Jebusite, Perizzite, and Hivite peoples. One of the most important, for the purposes of the narrative, is the nation called the Hivites. Their capital city was Gibeon, and numbered about thirty thousand inhabitants. This city of Gibeon was next in Joshua's line of march, and was a walled city, well defended and skillfully protected.

Among the reigning monarchs of these six nations was a crafty and able statesman whose name was Adoni-zedec, a man famed in his day not only for political craft but for military genius. He had been observing with deep concern the advance of Israel, and as he saw their invincible progress, he realized that no single nation of Canaan would be able to stand before them. So he called together the other five reigning kings and proposed a league of nations. This league was to be composed of the six remaining nations of Palestine, of which league Adoni-zedec was to be the head. The nations of Palestine eagerly accepted the proposal and the league of defense was formed.

May we pause to remind the reader that these ancients were real people. It is sometimes hard to understand that the people and nations that occur as names in old records were actual folks of flesh and blood as we are. They had the same ambitions, the same passions, pleasures, and sorrows that stir our feelings today. They lived and they died, they laughed and they wept, they worked and they rested, and they had the same problems to face that any nation faces today.

So the Hivites, stirred with concern behind their massive walls, were as excited by the thought of the coming siege and battle as would your city be today, if an alien army suddenly appeared on the horizon, threatening to loot and destroy your habitations. The history and the records of the Hivite people appear in the findings of archeology, where they are known as the Hovite nation. Adoni-zedec, the head of this ancient league of nations, was informed of the overthrow of the city of Jericho, and was possessed of the details of the capture of Ai. He knew that he faced a tremendous power. His strategy called for the sacrifice of the Hivites. He desired to use the city of Gibeon as a buffer between Israel and the rest of the league, while the army of the league took time to prepare for the defense of the rest of their territory.

We have often thought that this record should be a comfort to those courageous men who have kept our nation out of the present League of Nations. There is nothing new in the idea of the leagues of nations, for here is one that dates back almost thirty-five centuries. This league was organized to frustrate the people and the plan of God. It was headed by a man of worldly wisdom, who knew nothing of God and His will for the land wherein he dwelt. This land was foul with the most unnatural sins, and the only way the land could be purged was by the removal of the source of infection, which was the entire utterly degenerated populace.

So this league recognized no law save the law of expediency, and when its leader thought it desirable, he did not hesitate to sacrifice one entire nation. You may be sure that the nation elected to the sacrifice was not his own people! Adoni-zedec's strategy called for the fortification of his capital city, Jerusalem. In that region he intended to mass the combined army of the league, in the hope that he could crush Joshua in a pitched battle. So he called a secret meeting of his league and failed to inform the Hivites that the meeting was being held. With skillful oratory he told the fellow members something like this, "It is better that one should die for all, than that we should all perish together. We realize the seriousness of this decision, but it is necessary that somebody be sacrificed for the good of the league. The walls of Gibeon are strong and high, and they will delay Joshua long enough for us to complete our plans and fortifications. Therefore, we will betray our allies, the Hivites, and toss them to the lions to delay the onrush until we are ready for battle."

The rest of the league were sympathetic with the Hivites, but understood the brilliant strategy of Adoni-zedec. As long as they were not themselves to be the victims, they voted to have it that way. The Hivites, however, refused the role of martyr. They apparently had their spies at the conference of the league. When they learned that they were to be offered as a sacrifice for the rest of the league, they acted first. Promptly, they betrayed the pact before the pact could betray them! They perpetrated one of the shrewdest stratagems of history, and as a result gained a secret pact with Israel that made them servants of the God of Israel in return for protection and security.

It is not too much to say that the Hivites were probably the shrewdest people who ever lived on the face of this earth. In defense of that statement, we would offer the ingenious stratagem perpetrated by the Gibeonites, the story of which is told in the ninth chapter of Joshua, which chapter we are now discussing. Somewhere in their city these Gibeonites found some old gentlemen with frowsy hair and ragged white beards. They dressed them in worn-out garments and put upon their feet clouted and broken shoes. They provided these impostors with patched and mended wine-skins, in which they put a few pints of sour vinegar. They gave them some mouldy crusts of bread, and sent them forth as ambassadors of their mighty power.

Into the camp of the Children of Israel these humbugs limped, saying as they came, "We be come from a country that is very far removed. We have heard of the might of Israel and the power of thy God, and we have come to make a pact with thee."

The princes of Israel replied, "How do we know that you do not belong in this very land that we have set out to conquer?"

These skillful prevaricators humbly replied, "You see our worn-out shoes and clothing? These were our newest and best suits when we started on this long, hard journey. These wine-skins, now patched and broken, were new when we left home. They were filled with sweet grape-juice, and smell them now!" Displaying their mouldy crusts of bread, they shook their heads with sorrow and said, "Gentlemen, these were hot biscuits right out of the oven, when we started on this trip."

The record states that the princes of Israel were "convinced by the victuals," and they fell into this trap. They swore by the honor of Jehovah that they would never lift sword against the city of these ambassadors, but made with them a compact of peace and amity forever.

We had the audacity to maintain that the Hivites were the shrewdest people that ever lived. This seems reasonable in the face of the fact that they were the only people of history who have ever beaten all the Jews in a bargain at the same time! If the reader does not think that that requires brains, try it on one child of Abraham, and see how far you get!

When the ambassadors were rested, the journey of the horde was resumed, until they came before the walls of Gibeon. When the princes of Israel prepared the horde for the battle, they said to these mock-ambassadors, "Stand thou by and see how we overcome this city."

The ambassadors replied, "Not *this* city! This is *our* city, protected by your oath of friendship and peace."

The princes of Israel raved with indignation, but they were securely trapped, and saw no way out. So, characteristically, they made the best of a bad bargain and got what they could out of the deal. They bound the Gibeonites to themselves by an oath and said, "Thou shalt be the slaves of our God forever."

The Gibeonites retorted that it was better to be living slaves of a mighty God than dead re-jecters of a pact, and the covenant of mutual defense and protection was consummated. There being no further use for the army at the moment, Joshua marched the horde up to Gil-gal, where they went into rest camp to recover from the ravages of their hard campaigns.

When Adoni-zedec, the genius and head of the league, heard of the defection of the Hivites, he was alarmed as well as angered. He reasoned justly that if Israel added to their own army the thirty thousand fighting Hivites, the league was hopeless. Not only was the league weakened, but Israel was strengthened by this number. So he did the only logical thing under the circumstances, and called upon the rest of the heads to join him. He informed them of the defection of the Hivites and bitterly railed against their lack of faith and fidelity to the pact. It seems to have been all right, in his estimation, for the league to betray a member, but the member must not betray the league!

Gathering together the army of the five remaining nations, he planned to fall upon Gibeon and exterminate the Hivites. Thus he would not only punish their treachery to the league, but would at the same time destroy an added menace. He seems to have reasoned that they might successfully resist Joshua or overcome the Gibeonites separately, but that together the combination would be too strong. The king of the Hivites, however, seems to have kept a close watch upon the movements of the league, and his spies at once informed him of the coming of the punitive column. Fearing for the safety of his nation, he sent to Joshua, who was camped with the horde at Gilgal, and called for help. Joshua immediately answered, and after one of the most remarkable forced marches of history, Joshua's company flanked the army of the league. Thus, when the host under Adonizedec fell upon Gibeon, Joshua smote their rear and right flank. The Gibeonites made a sortie and attacked the head and the left flank of the column. Caught between the jaws of a pincer movement, the army of the league retreated across the plains of Beth-horon. The retreat soon turned into a rout, until with the Gibeonites pressing on one side and the Israelites on the other, the army of the five kings was utterly destroyed.

So much for the setting of the battle. Now let us look at the incidents of the battle itself. It is evident that the historical significance of the battle is usually forgotten and the event is now remembered almost solely because of the miracle of the long day that occurred in connection with that battle.

The higher critic still thinks that this is a weak spot in the Bible's claim to inspiration and infallibility. But then, if it were not for scholarly ignorance there would be no higher criticism, so we will meet their objections and show once more that the so-called "weak points" of the Bible are its strongest defense! This is the passage that is under critical assault:

"And it came to pass, as they fled from before Israel, and were in the going down to Beth-horon, that the Lord cast down great stones from heaven upon them unto Azekah, and they died; there were more which died from hailstones than they whom the children of Israel slew with the sword. Then spake Joshua to the Lord in the day when the Lord delivered up the Amorites before the children of Israel, and he said in the sight of Israel, Sun, stand thou still upon Gibeon, and thou, Moon in the Valley of Ajalon. And the sun stood still, and the moon stayed, until the people had avenged themselves upon their enemies. Is not this written in the Book of Jasher? So the sun stood still in the midst of heaven, and hasted not to go down about a whole day. And there was no day like it before it or after it, that the Lord hearkened to the voice of a man; for the Lord fought for Israel."

In these present days, long after all the witnesses are dead, the modernistic schools say that this is an impossible myth, and that such a thing never happened. To prove their case against this account, they advance three general objections.

The first one is that this account was not written by Joshua or any of his company, but was an interpolation by later writers. The critics seek to have us believe that some nameless scribe, more than a thousand years later than Joshua, added this story to the record that he was copying. As in all the modernistic efforts to simplify the Bible by removing its supposed mistakes and ruling out the miraculous, the explanation is worse than the so-called error! Not one iota of proof has ever been advanced by anyone to show that this was not in Joshua's original manuscript. The account itself, however, contains absolute and scientific evidence that this event *was recorded by an eye-witness!*

Let us look at certain statements in their relative order.

First, the sun was in the "midst" of the heavens. The word here translated "midst" is the Hebrew word "chatsi", which appears in the Old Testament 118 times. Of this number, it is translated 105 times by the English word "half". Its literal meaning is "bisection", and it implies that the sun was at the zenith. In other words, it was high noon.

Second, we note that while the sun was in the bisection of the heavens it stood over Gibeon! The sun was directly overhead in the center of the heaven, and right above the city of Gibeon. In the Palestinian summer the sun is between eight and twelve degrees of absolute zenith at noon. It then rises at five o'clock in the morning, and sets at seven o'clock in the evening.

Third, the city of Gibeon is in latitude thirty-one degrees and fifty-one minutes north. Remember this location, as it is of the utmost importance. If convenient, locate Gibeon on an old map, and see that this is so.

Fourth, the moon was in the Valley of Ajalon. The account does not say *over* the valley, but distinctly says *in* the valley. This valley was a low pass, or cleft in the hills. In the modern American West it would be called a "gun-sight pass." It was not a distinct valley, but a depression or canyon in the hills. As the declining moon touched the horizon, it would appear literally to be framed in the valley! This Valley of Ajalon lies seventeen degrees north of west from the city of Gibeon.

So if the sun was directly above Gibeon, and the moon was in the valley of Ajalon, the moon was in the third quarter on this day of battle and was setting at the time of the cry of Joshua. The moon then rose at eleven o'clock the night before the battle and set at one o'clock the battle day. At noon, when Joshua spoke his petition and cried out to God, the moon, which would disappear at an altitude of five degrees, was just at seven degrees altitude, or almost touching the horizon.

The day of the battle is thus established. It was July 22 by our calendar, or the twenty-first day of the fourth month by the Hebrew calendar. This month was called "Tammuz", and was composed of parts of our months of June and July. The sun's declension then was about twenty-one degrees north, and thus about eleven degrees from the absolute zenith. No unaided eye could tell this from the exact "middle", "half", or "chatsi" of the heavens! (This date is not given, of course, in the text, but it is a simple problem in chronology to figure it out from the data unconsciously given in this account of the battle.)

In the interesting study of this event which was made by Prof. Totten, he sought to show that this day covered the twenty-fourth and twenty-fifth days of the fourth civil month on the Hebrew calendar, and were the one hundred thirteenth and one hundred fourteenth calendar days. He sought to show the twenty-third day of that month was the winter solstice, and reckoning back from the autumn equinox of 1896, he showed that the battle day was 3370 solar years ago. But a factor of error entered into his calculations when he placed the moon *over the city* of Ajalon instead of *in the valley* that bore the same name.

The ancients kept astronomical records as far back as the third century before Christ. The Egyptians seem to have kept records only of the solstices, but the Chaldeans and other ancient people recorded cycles of eclipses, both lunar and solar, many of which records have been recovered by various expeditions. Disregarding calendar changes and dealing only with a chronology based upon solar motion, we go back to the earliest available records of the ancients and use them for a starting point. Carefully tracing up to Joshua's day of battle from the first and most accurate of those astronomical records, we arrive at the conclusion that the day of battle was *Tuesday.*

Then starting with the latest eclipse data of our year and reckoning our way back to that day of battle, we arrive at Wednesday. Deciding that we have made some sort of error in our conclusions, we go back and start again. We find that our first conclusion was right. When we check up from early data and arrive at this day of battle, it was what we would now call Tuesday, July 22.

Then we again check over our records from the year 1936 back to the time of Joshua's conquest, and once more we arrive at Wednesday, the twenty-second day of July. That is to say, the day of the month seems to be the same, but the day of the week is different.

Figuring any way that we can conceive, and using all of the information in the records of chronology, we find that there is a day missing in that week. In the record the exact relationships of the various solar factors are carefully noted, and by correlating these given positions, we are able to state the time and date of this battle.

Since this account does contain these solar factors, we have the confidence to maintain that it must have been written by an eye-witness. No later writer could have known this scientifically accurate combination of relative positions, until the modern science of astronomy was born. And no later "interpolater" could have guessed this, as this relative position is reached just once in each lunar cycle. So the sick, feeble theory of interpolation breaks down. It was at best only a poor crutch to support infidelity, but even that is gone.

The second objection of the critics is even weaker! Some of them contend that "this story of the long day is a pure myth, invented to clothe Joshua with a super-human character." Their argument here is ingenious. "The people," they explain, "still felt the loss of Moses. They had loved and followed him, and had seen how God had given him miracle-working power, and they were dubious about this new and youthful leader. So to give the people confidence in Joshua, this pleasing myth was invented to make him popular."

This sounds so smooth and plausible, it is almost a shame to examine it and see the truth! But like most of man's wisdom which seeks to discredit the Word of God, it fails of its purpose.

In the first place, it is not true that the people blindly loved and followed Moses! Was it not Moses whom they cast out, saying, "Who made *thee* to be a ruler and a judge over us?" To this same man they spoke in anger, "Better to have died in Egypt than to have followed you into this wilderness!" So deep was their injustice to Moses, that God at one time told Moses to separate himself from the tribes, that the Lord might sweep them out of existence! No, this people did not love and follow Moses in blind devotion, and as they were continually calling for a new leader, they should have been satisfied with Joshua. There was no need to glorify Joshua with "myths"; and if there had been, this account would not have sufficed.

If you read the account carefully, you will see that it is not Joshua who gets the glory, but God! All through the account of this miracle, the reader is impressed with one thing which the writer strives to emphasize. This central theme is not the glory of some human being, but rather the account impresses the reader with the wonder of the fact that God would hear and answer the cry of a man! And it is God's power and willingness to answer prayer that is the outstanding note in this account! If *you* by a word of command could lengthen the day, how would the modern chronicler write the event? The man who did it would get the glory, and the papers would be full of the man, man, man! If Joshua needed glorifying, this was a poor way to do it. The theory also fails to take note of the fact that the people whom Joshua led were all there when this miracle occurred, and no *fraudulent* claims would serve to elevate the new leader in their regard.

Parallel accounts in the records of other nations also prove that this account is not a myth. We have indisputable evidence from the modern science of ethnology that such an event occurred as Joshua records. Briefly we may summarize this section by saying that in the ancient Chinese writings there is a legend of a long day. The Incas of Peru and the Aztecs of Mexico have a like record, and there is a Babylonian and a Persian legend of a day that was miraculously extended. Another section of China contributes an account of the day that was miraculously prolonged, in the reign of Emperor Yeo. Herodotus recounts that the priests of Egypt showed him their temple records, and that there he read a strange account of a day that was twice the natural length. But how improbable these accounts all sound when compared with the true record in the Word of God! Let us look at one such instance, from the folk-lore of the Polynesians.

Maui was a great Polynesian character, who embodies some characteristics of the supernatural, according to the record of his many deeds. One of these great feats of Maui was his capture of the sun. The great god Kane had served notice on the mother of Maui that he and some lesser gods would visit her home and sup with her! Honored by this event, the woman began preparing a great feast for her celestial visitors. But as the day wore on, she saw she could not finish her tasks before the setting of the sun, so she appealed to her hero son for aid. Nothing daunted, Maui made a snare of coconut fibers, and climbing a high mountain, he lassoed the sun. Then he broke all its legs off, and the sun had to sit on top of the mountain until it grew a new set of legs! This took almost a whole day; and the mother of Maui had time and to spare in the preparation of the feast! Have you ever seen the long, slanting rays of light that shoot down from the sun in the late afternoon? To this very day, the Polynesians call those rays "The Snares of Maui"!

Is there any historical significance in these weird traditions and ancient accounts? Of course they are grossly exaggerated, but they do have this value: they show by their universal agreement that there is a basic truth behind them all! And this basic truth is the long day of Joshua. At the conclusion of this chapter we will seek to summarize the absolute and scientific proof that this account is not a myth. Let this suffice for the time. The event is substantiated by many parallel records, two of which we will note.

First, the reference in the text to the Book of Jasher. According to the traditions, a noted patriot, known as Jasher the Upright, gathered together a number of songs and poems, all commemorating great events in the history of Israel. The writer of Joshua calls attention to the fact that the miracle of the long day is preserved in the Book of Jasher the Upright.

We also have a reference to this event in the writing of Habakkuk, the prophet. In chapter three, verse eleven, the inspired man of God refers to this event as illustrating the wonderful power of a prayer-answering God. So the account is not a myth; it does stand alone.

Are the critics convinced? Not they! If they only desired to weigh evidence with clear understanding, they would not be critics! No man in full possession of average sense and all his faculties would criticize the Word of God! Driven from cover and confounded in his first arguments, he brings his last objection against the account, and says, "This is a scientific impossibility."

This generality is infidelity's commonest and greatest argument. Every callow student, every unbeliever in the seats of learning, and those who have read large volumes of certain types of pseudo-scientific literature, all advance this objection. We have often noticed that the less scientific learning the critic possesses, the quicker he is to advance this plea! For only the scientifically ignorant are scientifically dogmatic! There are three general scientific objections offered by this school, and we will take each in order.

The first is this: "Joshua told the sun and moon to stand still, while we know that the sun and moon do not move; it is the earth that moves around the sun. This language is quite natural to the day and time of Joshua; for he, of course, knew nothing of the theory of heliocentricity, and to his natural eye it looked as if the sun *did* move around the earth. But we know now that this is a scientific mistake, and an impossibility."

There is a profound and deep fallacy in all this reasoning of the critic. Or we should say, *two fallacies.* The first is the limitation of Joshua's knowledge. We do not know whether Joshua knew that our solar system is heliocentric or not, and it does not matter either way. For this account was not written out of Joshua's knowledge. It came by the inspiration of the Holy Ghost, Who used Joshua as a simple instrument to preserve the revelation in a written form, and He knows all things!

The second fallacy is the language ascribed to Joshua. Joshua did not say to the sun and moon, "Stand still!" You know, of course, that Joshua spoke in Hebrew, not in English, and this text was written in the Hebrew language. To get it into an English version, it had to be translated from the original. So before we criticize Joshua, let us look at his own language and see just what he did say. Out of this sentence under discussion, it will suffice to attract attention to just one Hebrew word. When Joshua spoke he said, "Sun, be thou 'damam' ".

The word "damam" appears in the Old Testament a total number of twenty-one times, and in no other single place is it translated "stand still". The word is the typical Hebrew equivalent of the English phrase, "be silent". The Hebrew word for "stand" is "amad." The word "amad" appears in the Old Testament many hundreds of times, and is consistently translated "stand" and "stand still". It occurs in this tenth chapter of Joshua, in the eighth verse, where God promises Joshua victory over his enemies, saying, "There shall not one of them stand (amad) before thee."

So when Joshua spoke to the sun, he said, "Sun, be thou silent." The marginal reading of every Bible in our personal possession gives this translation. Look in your own Bible and see what the margin says, just by way of confirmation. Now see the logic in this cry. Joshua didn't want more sunshine; sunshine was his great handicap!

Israel had made a magnificent forced march. They had started at Gilgal, and to get in behind the enemy and chase him away from his own cities and defenses, the army had marched more than forty miles in ten hours! They were loaded down with armor, spears, stones for the slings, bows, arrows, and all the accoutrements of ancient warfare. They had had no rest, and after this march of ten hours they began fighting. They fought about seven hours without rest, when the enemy broke and fled.

It was the twenty-second day of July, at noon. According to the average obtained from all the meteorological records ever kept in Palestine for this month of July, the thermometer registered between 105 and 120 degrees in the shade; and there was no shade for ten miles! The task of the army was the extermination of this allied host, and the host was in flight. The soldiers of Israel had marched all night—they had started fighting at the break of day—and it was high noon when the enemy broke and fled. They had had no rest or refreshment, and were exhausted by the hand to hand combat. The tired army of Israel, oppressed by the terrific heat, dropped in their places, and had no strength to run after a fleeing enemy. In this hour of extremity Joshua prayed, literally, "Hush up that sun!" ("Sun, be thou silent.")

The answer was instantaneous. A black cloud darkened the sun, and a storm of icy hail fell. And this in a season of the year when it never has been known to rain in Palestine! The first rains begin in our month of November with light thunder showers, and the last rains cease in April, again dying out with light showers. From December to February, twenty to thirty inches of rain will fall, but never a drop comes down in the summer season. On this occasion, however, in reply to Joshua's sudden cry for relief, the great shower of hailstones came. This was a two-fold answer; the air cooled and refreshed the army, and the hailstones slew the enemy.

The events of that day are evidently not given in their chronological order in the tenth chapter of Joshua. Verses seven to ten constitute a complete, abbreviated, epitomized record of the entire victory. Verses eleven to fifteen contain additional details added to the epitomized record, to bring a fuller illumination and add glory to the name of God. The chronology of the events of the battle can best be worked out by correlating the geographical positions of the points that are named, such as Beth-horon, Azekah, and Makkedah. So we have first of all the complete account of the success of the battle, and then a statement is made that in the course of the battle great hailstones fell upon the fleeing horde. Following that, the record is given as to why the hailstones came, namely, in response to the prayer of Joshua.

Now note that the text says that the sun was silenced, but it does not say that time ceased. It says, "The sun *hastened not* to go down. . ."

Time slowed down! In other words, time was prolonged.

Now we know that physical time is merely man's acquiescence to the mathematics of God. Our day, for instance, is just the space of hours and minutes it takes this earth to revolve on its axis one complete revolution. The mean average of all the year is exactly twenty-three hours, fifty-six minutes, four and nine-tenths seconds for each day. The earth keeps her schedule on her annual journey of five hundred and fifty million miles to such accuracy that she never varies as much as one one-hundredth of a second a year; and her daily rotation must be on the same plane of accuracy. It has been said that if this diurnal rotation had slowed down at the rate of one one-hundredth of a second each day, for just six thousand years, the day would now be more than thirty hours long, and the year would be composed of only two hundred and ninety-two of these days.

At any rate, the argument of infidelity totally collapses at every point, as Joshua did not say to the sun, "stand still", but "be silent", or "slow down." That this earth did at one time slow down will finally be shown from purely scientific grounds, in the last point of this present chapter.

The second scientific objection of the critics is equally fallacious. Driven from the previous point, the critic says, "The earth could neither stop nor slow down, as this is contrary to known law." To which we reply, "How much law do we know?"

We entered the office of a legal friend some time ago, and stood and wondered at the vast number of volumes of law that ringed his walls. This is a man of national prominence, who practices before the Supreme Court of the United States, and in one form of law only. Yet he had hundreds upon hundreds of books of law on his shelves.

There were thousands of laws therein, and we asked him, "Judge, how many of those laws do you know?"

To our surprise, he replied, "Oh, about fifty."

We said, "Then how can you practice with the many others?"

With a smile he replied, "Whenever a man comes in with a case, I listen to his side; then I say, 'Undoubtedly you have law on your side.' Then I take his money for a retaining fee and send him home while I look up the law that *is* on his side."

So then, law is modified by law!

The law of inertia is modified by the law of velocity. It is a fact that objects heavier than air cannot float through the air, but an airplane weighing tons will fly with ease if it has sufficient speed. We know so little of natural law that we cannot say what may be done and what is impossible, in this particular realm.

And there are higher laws of which we know nothing. We feel sure that what we call "miracles" are but orderly proceedings on the plane of higher laws, unknown to us, which are superior to the laws we do know. When the human voice comes from the horn of the phonograph, it is a "miracle" to the savage. We have evidence to show that the radio is a profound miracle to the untutored mind of the man of the wild estate; yet we know that these things are based upon laws that are above their present comprehension. There are also other laws that God knows and through which He works, that our darkened human minds do not yet comprehend!

Let us also contemplate another pertinent question, namely: *Who made this law or these laws!*

Law is predicated upon two postulates. The first requisite for law is a being or body of sufficient power to establish that law. The second essential is a being or body of sufficient power to enforce that law. So that if there *is* law in the natural world. behind that law is the Law-Maker and the Law-Enforcer. It goes without saying that the body that makes a law may rescind, amend, or retract that law.

But is this long day of Joshua contrary to known law? Is it lawfully impossible for this earth to have stopped or slowed down? There are exceptions to "natural law". We do not know much law, and what we do know may in almost every case be excepted.

As an instance, let us look at the mathematical law of the motion of satellites. This law may be stated thus: "All satellites advance from west to east around their primary bases."

The earth moves that way around the sun. The moon moves that way around the earth. Mars has two moons, and they and the parent planet move that way around the sun. Jupiter has five moons; they all advance that way around their parent planet. This is the established law of the satellites; that they must advance from west to east around their primary.

But the planet Uranus has four moons, all of which violate this law by retrograde motion! Instead of advancing from west to east, these four satellites advance from east to west, thus violating this "established law!"

No man knows a reason for this. In humorous moments we have sometimes thought that the Creator put these four satellites in reverse just to show us that He *has* a reverse gear, if He chooses to use it! Or that He wished to show that even if He established a law, He Himself was superior to that law, and could do the reverse if He so desired! This is a pleasing thought, and we chuckle whenever we contemplate it; but whatever the reason may be, here is an orderly established proceeding that *seems to be* contrary to natural law!

The long day of Joshua *may* be contrary to known law also, but there it is; it happened.

The final "scientific" argument of the critic is equally unavailing. It is a weak and ineffective bleat from the blind leaders of the sheep-like blind. When driven from every supposedly strong position, they say,

"Had there been such action as Joshua records, there would have been accompanying phenomena that would have left indelible record."

This is just contention, and we recognize it the more gladly because *there were just the phenomena demanded.* And they did leave their record.

First: the untimely and unseasonable storm of hail. This would be the first result to be expected in such an event.

Second: the darkness of the sun at midday.

Third: the lengthening of the day by half, which has left an incontrovertible and scientific record in the skies.

Summary: the writer concludes, "never was such a day seen before it or since, when the Lord fought for Israel."

In those words we have the answer to every question the human mind can raise.

The details are scarce. There is not room to comment on the event. But every question is answered there before it rises in that one trenchant sentence, "God fought for Israel'.' It was simply divine interposition.

The final testimony of science is that such a day left its record for all time. As long as time shall be, the record of this long day must remain. The fact is attested by eminent men of science, two of whom I quote here.

Sir Edwin Ball, the great British astronomer, found that twenty-four hours had been lost out of solar time. Where did that go, what was the cause of this strange lapse, and how did it happen? The answer may be expected in vain from sources of human wisdom and learning!

There is a place, however, where the answer is found. And this place is attested by a scientist of standing. There is a book by Prof. C. A. Totten of Yale, written in 1890, which establishes the case beyond the shadow of a doubt. The condensed account of his book, briefly summarized, is as follows:

Professor Totten wrote of a fellow-professor, an accomplished astronomer, who made the strange discovery that the earth was twenty-four hours out of schedule! That is to say, there had been twenty-four hours lost out of time. In discussing this point with his fellow-professors, Professor Totten challenged this man to investigate the question of the inspiration of the Bible. He said, "You do not believe the Bible to be the Word of God, and I do. Now here is a fine opportunity to prove whether or not the Bible is inspired. You begin to read at the very beginning and read as far as need be, and see if the Bible can account for your missing time."

The astronomer accepted the challenge and began to read. Some time later, when the two men chanced to meet on the campus, Professor Totten asked his friend if he had proved the question to his satisfaction. His colleague replied, "I believe I have definitely proved that the Bible is not the Word of God. In the tenth chapter of Joshua, I found the missing twenty-four hours accounted for. Then I went back and checked up on my figures, and found that at the time of Joshua there were only twenty-three hours and twenty minutes lost. If the Bible made a mistake of forty minutes, it is not the Book of God!"

Professor Totten said, "You are right, in part at least. But does the Bible say that a *whole day* was lost at the time of Joshua?" So they looked and saw that the text said, "*about* the space of a whole day."

The word "about" changed the whole situation, and the astronomer took up his reading again. He read on until he came to the thirty-eighth chapter of the prophet Isaiah. In this chapter, Isaiah has left us the thrilling story of the king, Hezekiah, who was sick unto death. In response to his prayer, God promised to add fifteen more years to his life. To confirm the truth of His promise, God offered a sign. He said, "Go out in the court and look at the sundial of Ahaz. I will make the shadow on the sundial back up ten degrees!" Isaiah recounts that the king looked, and while he looked, the shadow turned backward ten degrees, by which ten degrees it had already gone down! This settles the case, for ten degrees on the sundial is forty minutes on the face of the clock! So the accuracy of the Book was established to the satisfaction of this exacting critic.

When the astronomer found his day of missing time thus accounted for, he laid down the Book and worshipped its Writer, saying, "Lord, I believe!"

Search the heavens, for the truth is there. As long as the stars shall shine, as long as the earth shall spin, as long as time shall last, the long day of Joshua will be attested as a scientific fact!

Search the heavens indeed, but search the written Word as well! *The heavens only testify to those who have seen first the testimony of the Word!* For though the words and the works of God agree, the Word is high above the works, and when works shall melt and pass away, the Word shall forever endure.